# The Writer's Studio

Level B

## Lesli J. Favor, Ph.D.

Amsco School Publications, Inc.
315 Hudson Street
New York, N.Y. 10013

## About the Author

**Lesli J. Favor** holds a Ph.D. in English from the University of North Texas. After graduating, she was assistant professor of English at Sul Ross State University Rio Grande College, in southwest Texas. She left that position to write full-time. She has written twelve English/language arts books and coauthored three more, all for Amsco School Publications. In addition, she has written twelve nonfiction books for middle school and high school readers. She lives near Seattle with her husband, young son, two dogs, and horse.

## Consultant: Cathleen Greenwood

Cathleen Greenwood is an award-winning teacher, writer, and veteran presenter at national and local conferences on teaching and writing. She has written two books for teachers and has co-authored a book for young adults on writing. In addition, she has published poems, short stories, and essays in magazines and journals. She is a consultant for the National Council of Teachers of English (NCTE) and a judge for the NCTE Promising Young Writers award program. She teaches at Rippowam Cisqua School in Bedford, New York.

## Reviewers:

**Robert Gath**, 8th-Grade Literature/Language Arts Teacher and English Department Head, Simmons Middle School, Oak Lawn, Illinois

**Ivana Orloff**, English Teacher and English Language Arts Standards Review Course Lead, Whittier High School, Whittier, California

**Gary Pankiewicz**, Supervisor of English Language Arts (6–12), District of South Orange and Maplewood, New Jersey, and adjunct writing instructor at Montclair State University

Cover Design: Armen Kojoyian
Cover Photo: Copyright © istockphoto.com/zentilia
Text Design: Delgado & Company
Composition: Publishing Synthesis, Ltd., New York
Graphic Art: Hadel Studio
Illustrations: Clive Goodyer (Beehive Illustration)

Please visit our Web site at: *www.amscopub.com*

When ordering this book, please specify:
*either* **R 174 P** *or* THE WRITER'S STUDIO, LEVEL B.

ISBN: 978-1-56765-204-8 / *NYC Item 56765-204-7*

Copyright © 2011 by Amsco School Publications, Inc.

1  2  3  4  5  6  7  8  9  10          16  15  14  13  12  11

# Contents

# Welcome to *The Writer's Studio*

A studio is a place where an artist develops a craft or skill. A photographer develops prints, a dancer practices a routine, a singer records an album, and a writer composes a story. Think of this book as *your* writing studio—a place where you will develop as a unique and skilled writer. As you work through this book, you'll learn about a variety of genres (kinds) of writing, examine model essays, and practice writing for a variety of audiences and purposes. You'll also learn how to add your own creativity and self-expression to your writing. Just like fingerprints, no two writers are alike. Your writing rings with your voice, your style, your experiences, and your perspective. The unique place you come from as a writer can help you succeed in this literary craft.

Take a moment to review where you stand as a writer. Complete the following activity. Your teacher may ask you to share your responses in a class discussion.

## What Do You Think About Writing?

Read each of the following statements. Decide whether you strongly agree, strongly disagree, or stand somewhere in between. Then draw an X to mark your position on the scale.

1. Strong writers are born that way.

   strongly agree                    strongly disagree

2. Writing is useful for school, but it's not very useful beyond that.

   strongly agree                    strongly disagree

3. Strong writers usually get the words down right the first time, without needing to revise or get feedback.

strongly agree — strongly disagree

4. A writer should never write in the first person (use *I*).

strongly agree — strongly disagree

5. As long as your ideas are good, it doesn't matter if you follow the rules of punctuation and grammar.

strongly agree — strongly disagree

As you complete each unit in this book, take a moment to return to these questions. Think about whether the placement of each X still represents your beliefs about writing. If necessary, mark an X for deletion and write a new X to show your current position.

## Your Writers' Network

The British poet John Donne wrote, "No man is an island, entire of itself; every man is a piece of the continent, a part of the main." Similarly, no writer is an island, working entirely alone. Each writer is a part of a larger group. For instance, writers in the workplace and professional writers turn to peers, editors, or a writers' group for feedback and encouragement.

Whom do you know who could become part of your own writers' network? In the box on the next page, write the names and contact information of at least three people who will form your network. Make sure that one of them is a classmate in this class.

## Why Study Writing?

The ability to write clearly and engagingly in a variety of genres is a sure sign of a solid education. It prepares you for success in school, in college, and beyond in careers and daily life. For this reason, students are asked to demonstrate their ability in various forms of writing. These forms, or genres, include descriptive, expository, persuasive, and literary writing as well as response to literature. Classroom tests, state tests, the SAT, and the ACT measure your ability to write clear, original, well-organized paragraphs and essays.

Teachers and other educators who evaluate your writing will check to see how well you use certain *traits of writing*. The following table explains six important traits.

# Six Traits of **Writing**

| Ideas | The writing is clear and focused. Each detail clearly relates to the topic. |
|---|---|
| Organization | Details are arranged in a logical manner, such as from least to most important or in chronological order. |
| Voice | The writer shines through as a real person behind the writing. The writing style fits with the purpose and audience of the piece. |
| Word Choice | Words are vivid and accurate, helping to draw in the reader while making ideas clear. |
| Sentence Fluency | A variety of sentence types and structures creates a pleasing rhythm to the writing. |
| Conventions | Capitalization, spelling, punctuation, and grammar are correct. |

These six traits of writing form the backbone of the lessons in the books in this series.

## About This Series

This is the second book of *The Writer's Studio*, a three-volume writing instruction series. *Level A* provides instruction, review, and practice in five important genres of writing. In this book, *Level B*, you'll sharpen your writing skills and increase your knowledge of the traits of writing. In *Level C*, you'll continue to strengthen your writing in different genres while learning more sophisticated writing skills and techniques. All three levels contain detailed sections on test writing to help you prepare for writing in different genres on school, state, and national tests.

# What's Inside This Book

*The Writer's Studio, Level B* contains a variety of lessons, features, and activities.

**Unit Opener:** This section introduces you to a particular genre of writing and shows you why the genre is important.

> **Six Traits of Writing:** For each unit, the table of writing traits is tailored to explain a specific genre of writing.

> **Real-World Examples:** These are short models of writing taken from books and Web sites. They show how writers use a particular genre outside the classroom.

> **Learning Tips:** These are suggestions for linking your classroom study to your life outside of school.

**Rubrics:** Each chapter includes a 4-point rubric, or scoring guideline, tailored for a specific genre of writing.

**Models:** In each chapter, one model of writing helps to teach the traits of writing. A second model provides an opportunity for you to use the rubric to evaluate the strength of your writing.

**Writer's Toolkit** and **Tips:** Strategies and tips for the stages of the writing process.

**Checklists:** Revising and editing checklists in each chapter help you improve your work.

**Mini-Lessons:** These lessons target some of the trouble spots that face writers. Topics range from grammar to sentence structure to thesis statements.

**Test Writing:** These chapters prepare you for writing tasks on school, state, and national tests.

**Unit Wrap-Up:** In this section you will summarize and reflect on what you have learned.

> **You Be the Judge:** You will evaluate an essay that was written by a real student.

**Ideas for Writing:** This is a bank of additional writing prompts from which you or your teacher can choose. One choice asks you to Write Across the Curriculum, using information from a subject such as social studies or science.

**Reflections:** In a graphic organizer, you will organize your thoughts, accomplishments, and goals regarding a genre of writing.

**Conventions Handbook:** Rules and definitions of key terms in the areas of sentences, the eight parts of speech, how words work in sentences, and punctuation.

This book is a valuable resource that will help you become a stronger writer in many different genres and writing situations. Complete the series, and you'll see big improvements in your ability to write clearly, powerfully, and engagingly.

Good luck!

Lesli J. Favor, Ph.D., *Author*

# Descriptive Writing

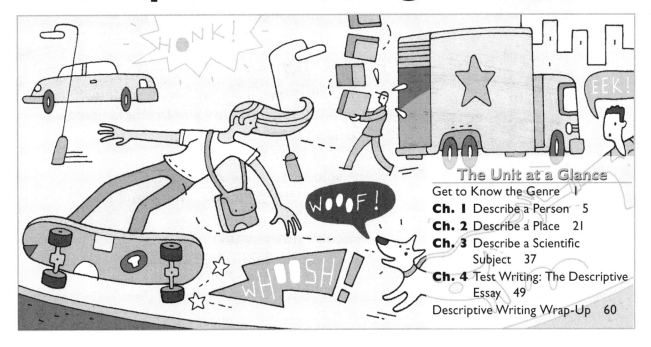

## Get to Know the Genre: Descriptive Writing

In many ways, large and small, we use descriptions to connect to people around us. We ask and answer questions such as these:

*What did your friend's face look like when you jumped out and yelled, "Surprise"?*

*How will I know which house is yours?*

*What does your new dog look like?*

*What was it like to watch a live ice hockey match?*

In answering questions like these, you use descriptive details to bring something to life for someone else. In the same way, you can bring people, places, things, and experiences to life in descriptive writing.

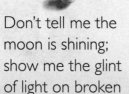

Don't tell me the moon is shining; show me the glint of light on broken glass.
—Anton Chekhov *(Russian playwright and short-story writer, 1860–1904)*

Descriptive writing tells about a person, place, thing, or experience in a way that helps readers connect to the subject as though they were right there. Sensory details—those that appeal to sight, hearing, taste, touch, and smell—help to do this.

## Give It a Try: Explore Sensory Details

On separate paper, complete each sentence.
1. A smell that I sometimes notice at school is…
2. I couldn't help staring when I saw…
3. The best taste in the world is…
4. The sole of my shoe feels like…
5. At 6:00 P.M. in my house, you would hear…

On page xii of this book's introduction, you read about six traits of writing. Now look at the table below. It shows how these traits link to descriptive writing.

## Six Traits of Descriptive Writing

| Ideas | The topic is narrowed to a specific person, place, thing, or experience. Each detail clearly relates to the topic. |
|---|---|
| organization | Details are arranged with care, such as from least to most important or in time order. |
| voice | The writer shines through as a real person behind the writing. The writing style fits with the purpose and audience of the description. |
| word choice | Nouns, adjectives, adverbs, and verbs are specific and lively. Sensory details bring life to sights, sounds, textures, smells, and/or tastes. |
| sentence fluency | A variety of sentence types and structures creates a pleasing rhythm to the writing. |
| conventions | Capitalization, spelling, and punctuation are correct. |

## Real-World Example

You've reviewed the traits of descriptive writing. Now read this descriptive paragraph from the novel *Hatchet* by Gary Paulsen. The book is about a boy who is stranded in the wilderness after a plane crash. He survives alone for nearly two months before being rescued. The paragraph below describes Brian's face-to-face encounter with a black bear.

> **Ideas:** The paragraph describes one specific experience.
>
>      The sun caught the ends of the hairs along his back. Shining black and silky the bear stood on its hind legs, half up, and studied Brian, just studied him, then lowered itself and moved slowly to the left, eating berries as it rolled along, Wuffling and delicately using its mouth to lift each berry from the stem, and in seconds it was gone. Gone, and Brian still had not moved. His tongue was stuck to the top of his mouth, the tip half out, his eyes were wide and his hands were reaching for a berry.
>
> **Word choice:** Vivid words appeal to the senses of sight, touch, and hearing.
>
> **Sentence variety:** A short sentence comes between two longer sentences.
>
> **Organization:** Actions are arranged in chronological order.

## Give It a Try: Examine the Real-World Example

Can you find additional examples of the six traits of writing in the model paragraph above? On separate paper, list two traits of strong descriptive writing. For each one, quote or describe an example from the model.

## Get Ready to Write

Now that you've explored the qualities of descriptive writing, you're ready to create some descriptions of your own. In the chapters that follow, you'll describe a person with inner or outer beauty, a favorite place to eat, and a useful machine or device. You'll also write a description of your ideal bedroom. You'll use the stages of the writing process—prewriting, drafting, revising, editing, and publishing—and you'll be presented with models and mini-lessons along the way.

As you work through these chapters, you can enrich your understanding by trying the suggestions below. These tips will help you connect what you're learning in this unit to your own life and the world around you.

---

### LEARNING TIPS

- Watch for descriptive writing in the reading you do for school. Think about how descriptive writing helps you understand ideas in math, science, and social studies.

- Listen for descriptions in people's conversations, and listen for descriptions in TV or radio commercials. When you hear a description, use it to create a mental image. Think about how you could make the description stronger.

- Watch for descriptive writing in magazines, in stories, in e-mails, and on menus. Think about the purpose of these descriptions. How does the writer seem to want the reader to respond?

- Practice writing—and speaking—descriptively. Write e-mails and make phone calls simply to describe something to someone. Use descriptions to strengthen your writing for other classes.

---

# Describe a Person

There are a lot of proverbs, or common sayings, about beauty. Here are a few:

*Beauty is as beauty does.*

*Beauty is only skin deep.*

*Beauty is in the eye of the beholder.*

What is your idea of beauty? As you sit in a crowded room, what qualities attract your attention to a specific person? Once you get to know someone, what qualities make you think the person is beautiful—inside and out? This chapter will give you an opportunity to explore your ideas of beauty. At the same time, you'll continue to build your skills of written description.

To get started, study this table. It tells how to use the traits of writing to compose strong, interesting descriptions of people.

## Six Traits of **Describing a Person**

| | |
|---|---|
| Ideas | The topic is narrowed to a specific person. Each detail clearly relates to this person. |
| organization | Details are arranged in a logical order, such as from least to most important. |
| voice | The writer shines through as a real person behind the writing. The writing style fits with the purpose and audience of the description. |
| word choice | The writer uses specific and lively words to bring the subject to life. |
| sentence fluency | A variety of sentence types and structures creates a pleasing rhythm to the writing. |
| conventions | Capitalization, spelling, and punctuation are correct. |

In the model paragraph below, the writer describes her friend Ethan and shows why he is beautiful.

> Ethan is a typical teenage guy with shaggy hair, braces on his teeth, and big, awkward feet. So what makes him beautiful? It's not the glossy sheen to his hair or the friendly smile on his face. It's not that he moves like magic on a dance floor. Instead, it is all of these characteristics added together, and more. Ethan is the kind of guy who can win a competition gracefully--or lose just as gracefully. He is kind to his little sister, and he shows respect to his parents. At the same time, he has a mischievous side to him that leads to water-balloon fights, practical jokes, and the occasional food fight. Ethan is beautiful because he is completely himself, inside and out.

## Give It a Try: Examine the Model Paragraph

Use the model paragraph above to answer the following questions. Write your answers on separate paper. Then, in a class discussion, explain your answers.

1. **Ideas.** Why do you think the writer asks a question in the second sentence?
2. **Organization.**
    a. What part of the paragraph gives physical details about Ethan?
    b. What part of the paragraph gives details about Ethan's personality?
    c. Copy the sentence that forms the transition between these parts of the paragraph.

3. **Voice and word choice.** List three words or phrases that catch your attention and make you feel as if a real person is writing this paragraph.

4. **Sentence fluency.** Copy the last sentence in the paragraph. Then underline the subordinate clause in this complex sentence.

5. **Conventions.** Copy the sentence that begins, "At the same time . . ." Then circle each comma in the sentence. In the class discussion, explain why each comma is there.

## Your Turn to Write: Describe a Person

Now you'll write your own decription of someone you know. Read the assignment carefully and follow the strategies and instructions for each stage of the writing process.

## Assignment

An old proverb states, "Beauty is in the eye of the beholder." The proverb means that each of us sees beauty in different people for different reasons. Physical characteristics such as eyes or hair may help to make someone beautiful. Or it may be inner traits such as kindness, humor, or compassion. Who is beautiful to you?
Write one paragraph of 100–150 words in which you describe what makes a specific person beautiful to you. Be sure to use sensory details to help your reader "see" this person. You are writing for an audience of classmates, so if you want to keep this person's identity a secret, you do not have to use the person's real name.

Prewrite

**Analyze the Prompt.** Reread the assignment closely and answer the following questions. Write your answers on separate paper.

1. What is the purpose of this paragraph?
2. Who is the audience for this paragraph?
3. How long does the paragraph need to be?

**Choose a Topic.** In each section of the table below, write the name of one person who is beautiful to you. Under each name, list a few details about the person's beauty. Finally, draw a star next to the name of the person who would make the best subject for your descriptive paragraph.

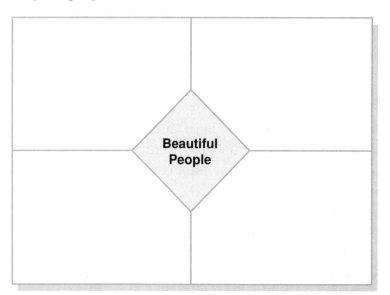

**Gather Ideas and Details.** Use the following table to jot down details about the person you chose to write about. Some details have been filled in as examples.

**Descriptive Details About** _____ (the name of your person)

| Concrete Details (physical qualities) | Abstract Details (personality traits) | Other Details (talents, actions, etc.) |
|---|---|---|
| large, dark eyes | generous to others | plays the piano beautifully |
| | | |

**Organize Ideas and Details.** Decide how you will arrange ideas and details in your description. Remember that the purpose of the paragraph is to describe what makes a specific person beautiful to you. Here are two methods of organization that work well in this type of description.

- **Group details by category.** As in the model paragraph about Ethan, group the descriptive details by category. For instance, categories can include concrete details, abstract details, and other categories such as sound details (for instance, if the person's singing ability is a big part of his or her beauty).

- **Order of importance.** Include details from least to most important. For example, start with the least important detail of beauty and build up to the detail that stands out to you the most.

**Organize Your Description.** Follow these four steps.

1. Review the details that you recorded in the Descriptive Details table above.

2. Circle the strongest details. These may be in one, two, or all three columns of the table.

3. Choose one of the organization methods described on the previous page. Write the name of the method.

4. List details in the order in which you will present them, based on your answer in step 3.

 Draft

Now it's time to get your ideas on paper in a paragraph format. As you know, the building blocks of a strong paragraph are a topic sentence, body sentences, and a closing sentence.

The **topic sentence** introduces the subject of your description in a way that hooks the reader's interest. For example, hook readers with an attention-getting physical detail or an unusual personality trait. Here are two examples.

> Ethan is a typical teenage guy with shaggy hair, braces on his teeth, and big, awkward feet. So what makes him beautiful? (The hook: Readers want to know how an average-looking guy can be beautiful.)

> Fairy tales are full of evil, ugly stepsisters, but my stepsister, Amanda, is the most beautiful girl I know. (The hook: Readers are drawn in by the contrast between evil fairy-tale sisters and the real-life stepsister, Amanda.)

Each of these examples introduces a specific person in a catchy way that makes the reader want to know more. At the same time, the purpose for writing—describing why the person is beautiful—is clear.

**Write Your Topic Sentence.** On separate paper, write a topic sentence for your paragraph.

Now read what you wrote. What do you think of your first effort? Want to try a different way of opening the paragraph? Write another topic sentence, and this time use a different attention-getting detail.

The **body sentences** of your paragraph build on the image that the topic sentence introduced. This part of the paragraph brings your subject (the person) to life. In the sentences below, the writer continues building a mental image of Amanda, the beautiful stepsister. Her description uses vivid word choices and relevant, interesting details.

**Organization:** This phrase lets the reader know that the details are arranged from least to most important.

At first, I noticed small things about Amanda. She has large, dark eyes that sparkle like gems. She also has wavy brown hair, and her hands have the long, graceful fingers of a natural-born piano player. Once I got to know Amanda better, I noticed that her beauty is not just skin deep. With her friendly nature, she attracts people like bees to honey. In addition, she is just as generous and good-natured around family members as she is around friends at school. Most important of all, Amanda has treated me with respect and affection since our parents got married. It was not easy for her to let me, a younger stepsister, move in and share her room. But Amanda welcomed me.

**Word choice:** vivid description

**Word choice:** transition

**Ideas:** Relevant examples (which have been circled) support the statement that Amanda is beautiful.

**Organization:** Details are arranged from least to most important.

**Write the Paragraph's Body Sentences.** Look back at the Organize Your Description task on pages 9 and 10. There, you listed details of your description in a logical order. Use this list to write the body of your paragraph on a separate sheet of paper.

The paragraph's **closing sentence** brings the description to an end. A strong closing sentence reinforces your opinion about the person's beauty.

In a one-paragraph description, the closing sentence can be simple and brief. It should not overshadow the body sentences by being long and detailed. And it should not simply repeat the topic sentence. Instead, it should summarize the overall impression of the person.

Here is the closing sentence for the paragraph about Amanda. In it, the writer reminds the reader that she has given examples of outside and inside beauty.

Outside and inside, she is beautiful.

**Write Your Closing Sentence.** Follow the steps below.

1. On separate paper, write a sentence that could bring your description to an end.

2. What do you think of your first effort? Could this sentence be more direct? Does it bring up new material instead of bringing old material to a close? Try writing another, different closing sentence.

3. Now write a clean copy of your entire paragraph, including the topic sentence, the body sentences, and the closing sentence of your choice.

 **Revise**

When you wrote the rough draft of your paragraph, you focused on getting your ideas down on paper. Now you will revise your paragraph to make it stronger. One way of making your paragraph stronger is to revise it for sentence fluency. The mini-lesson on the next page will show you how.

# Mini-Lesson: Sentence Fluency

*Sentence fluency* refers to the rhythm and flow of the sentences in a paragraph. A well-written paragraph has a pleasing rhythm when you read it aloud or silently. The writer uses a mix of short and long sentences and a variety of sentence types.

The first draft of your paragraph may contain many short, simple sentences. These sentences may be written correctly. However, too many simple sentences can create a choppy or repetitive rhythm. The sentences don't flow fluidly (smoothly). One strategy for adding sentence fluency is to combine two *simple sentences* into one *complex sentence*.

→ A **simple sentence** has one subject and one verb. It is a main (independent) clause.

> She has large, dark eyes.
> They sparkle like gems.

In the examples above, each subject is underlined once and each verb is underlined twice.

→ A **complex sentence** has one main clause and one or more subordinate clauses.

She has large, dark eyes **that** sparkle like gems.

In the complex sentence above, the main clause is underlined once. The subordinate clause is underlined twice. Notice that the word *that* begins the subordinate clause. This word is called a *subordinating conjunction*.

→ A **subordinating conjunction** is a word that begins a subordinate clause. Commonly used subordinating conjunctions include these:

| | | | | |
|---|---|---|---|---|
| after | because | so that | till | when |
| although | before | than | unless | whenever |
| as | if | that | until | where |
| as if | since | though | while | wherever |

## Give It a Try: Combine Simple Sentences to Form Complex Sentences

In each item below, combine the short, choppy sentences to form a complex sentence. To join the sentences, use a subordinating conjunction from the list at the bottom of page 13. Write your answers on separate paper.

1. I like her smile. It is wide and happy.

2. Her eyes are so dark brown. They look black.

3. She taps her foot. She waits for the bus.

4. I ate ice cream. I ate a cheeseburger.

5. I hung up my wet bathing suit. It will be dry this afternoon.

## Give It a Try: Revise Your Paragraph for Sentence Fluency

Revise the rough draft of your descriptive paragraph, looking for short, choppy sentences that give related ideas. Use subordinating conjunctions to create more pleasing complex sentences.

**Revise Your Paragraph for the Six Traits.** Following is a checklist that will help you decide what to change, remove, or leave in place. The Descriptive Paragraph Rubric that follows the checklist will help you determine how strong your paragraph is and where to make your revisions.

## Ideas

- ❏ Place a check mark next to your topic sentence if it introduces the person in a way that gets your reader's attention. If not, revise the sentence to make it more interesting.
- ❏ Underline three details and ideas that help to describe the person. Cross out any irrelevant details.

## Organization

- ❏ Check that your descriptive details are arranged in a logical order. Move any details that seem out of place.

## Voice

- ❏ Does your writing style fit with your audience (classmates)?
- ❏ Do you let your attitude or opinion about the person shine through? Write *voice* above two words or phrases that show your attitude or opinion.

## Word choice

- ❏ Circle three specific and expressive words you use to describe the person.

## Sentence fluency

- ❏ Check for a variety of sentence lengths and sentence types. Combine or shorten sentences if necessary.

# Descriptive Paragraph Rubric

| | 4<br>Strong | 3<br>Effective | 2<br>Developing | 1<br>Beginning |
|---|---|---|---|---|
| Ideas | One subject is described. Each detail clearly relates. | The subject is clear, but some details do not relate. | The writer is beginning to make the subject clear. | The subject is not clear. Most details do not relate. |
| organization | Supporting details are arranged logically. | Most details are arranged logically. | Organization of details is awkward. | Details are in random order. |
| voice | The writing style is distinctive and helps the reader connect to the description. | The writing style draws the reader in to the description but doesn't have a personal flair. | The writing style of one or two sentences, but not all, draws in the reader. | Writing is plain or dry, making it hard for readers to connect to the description. |
| word choice | Specific and lively words bring the subject to life. | Many words are specific and lively. | Words are simple but mostly correct. | Vocabulary is limited. |
| sentence fluency | A variety of sentence types is used in a pleasing rhythm. | A variety of sentence types is used, but some may be awkward. | Sentences are complete but are mostly short and simple. | Sentences are mostly of one type or are incomplete. |
| conventions | Capitalization, spelling, punctuation, and grammar are correct. | There are few errors in capitalization, spelling, punctuation, and grammar. | There are many errors in capitalization, spelling, punctuation, and grammar. | Errors in conventions make it hard to understand the writing. |

# Edit

To edit your writing means to find and correct mistakes in capitalization, spelling, punctuation, and grammar. You may or may not recognize each mistake right away. However, by using reference tools, outside feedback, and a self-tracking system, you can develop a reliable method for editing your work.

**Use reference tools.** If you are unsure of a word's spelling, use a dictionary. If you are unsure of capitalization or punctuation rules, use a handbook of conventions and rules.

**Get feedback.** Ask a classmate, family member, or tutor to circle mistakes in your writing. Then use reference tools to figure out how to correct the mistakes.

**Learn from your work.** As you correct mistakes, make sure you understand *why* something was a mistake. By learning the rules of conventions, you will begin to find and correct mistakes more quickly and easily.

**Edit Your Paragraph.** Edit the revised copy of your descriptive paragraph. The following questions will help you decide what to change, remove, or leave in place.

### Conventions
- ❑ Did you capitalize proper nouns, such as the subject's name?
- ❑ Did you use a comma when you joined sentences with a coordinating conjunction?
- ❑ Did you use a comma when you began a sentence with an introductory word, phrase, or clause?
- ❑ Did you correct spelling mistakes, either with a friend's help or by using a dictionary?
- ❑ Did you correct grammar mistakes, either with a friend's help or by using a grammar handbook?

**PUBLISH**

   **Presentation.** Prepare your descriptive paragraph for publication by neatly writing or typing the final, edited copy.

   **Publish Your Paragraph.** Here are a few ideas for publishing your descriptive paragraph.

- ❏ Give a copy to the person whom you described in the paragraph.
- ❏ With your teacher's permission, use an empty bulletin board to create a Board of Beauty. Hang a copy of your paragraph next to your classmates' work. Take the time to read what others have written.
- ❏ Paste a copy in your scrapbook alongside a photograph of the person you described.

## Evaluate Your Paragraph

Your teacher will either assess your paragraph, ask you to self-assess your paragraph, or ask you to switch with a partner and assess each other's work.

## Evaluate the Model Paragraph

Work with a partner to evaluate the following descriptive paragraph. Use the rubric on page 16 and write your score here: _____ . In a class discussion, explain the score you gave.

Fairy tales are full of evil, ugly stepsisters, but my stepsister, Amanda, is the most beautiful girl I know. At first, I noticed small things about Amanda. She has large, dark eyes that sparkle like gems. She also has wavy brown hair, and her hands have the long, graceful fingers of a natural-born piano player. Once I got to know Amanda better, I noticed that her beauty is not just skin deep. With her friendly nature, she attracts people like bees to honey. In addition, she is just as generous and good-natured around family members as she is around friends at school. Most important of all, Amanda has treated me with respect and affection since our parents got married. It was not easy for her to let me, a younger stepsister, move in and share her room. But Amanda welcomed me. Outside and inside, she is beautiful.

# Describe a Place

When you describe people, places, and other subjects, you share your own special perspective on these things. You help your readers stand in your shoes and look through your eyes. By choosing which details to include and which ones to leave out, you create a unique image, like a painting, that no one else can copy. In this chapter, you will practice "painting" an image of a favorite place.

Begin by examining the table below. Some information in the table will be familiar to you from Chapter 1. Some new details have been added to link to this chapter's topic—describing a place—and to the essay format.

## Six Traits of Describing a Place

| | |
|---|---|
| Ideas | The topic is narrowed to a specific place. Each detail clearly relates to this place. |
| organization | The essay includes an introduction that catches the reader's interest, body paragraphs that describe the place, and a conclusion that brings the description to a satisfying close. Ideas and details are arranged logically. |
| voice | The writer shines through as a real person behind the writing. The writing style fits with the purpose and audience of the description. |
| word choice | Nouns, adjectives, adverbs, and verbs are specific and lively. Sensory details are present. |
| sentence fluency | A variety of sentence types and structures creates a pleasing rhythm to the writing. |
| conventions | Capitalization, spelling, punctuation, and grammar are correct. |

In the model paragraph below, the writer describes her favorite place to eat.

The instant you step into La Canasta, you know that you are about to enjoy a rich dining experience. The scent of Mexican herbs and spices wafts toward you. Savory cumin blends with the sharper scents of cilantro and onion. In the lobby, Mexican souvenirs decorate the walls. Delicate hand-painted figurines sit on glass shelves, and pounded-silver frames hold mirrors. Red and blue sombreros hang over the arched entry to the dining room. In the center of the dining room, the heart of La Canasta, a fountain splashes gently. Around it sit carved wooden tables and chairs. As you slide into a red velvet-cushioned chair, a waiter greets you with a basket of hot, salty tortilla chips and the word "*Bienvenida*" (welcome). As Mexican music plays in the background, you settle in to study the menu. You know you won't be disappointed.

## Give It a Try: Examine the Model Paragraph

Use the model paragraph above to answer the following questions. Write your answers on separate paper. Then, in a class discussion, explain your answers.

1. **Ideas.** What place does the writer describe?
2. **Organization.** What method does the writer use to organize details (such as most to least important, spatial order, time order)? How can you tell?
3. **Voice.** Which point of view does the writer mainly use?

a. first-person point of view, which uses first-person pronouns such as *I*, *me*, and *my*

b. second-person point of view, which uses second-person pronouns such as *you* and *your*

c. third-person point of view, which uses third-person pronouns such as *he*, *she*, and *their*

4. **Word choice.** List three details that appeal to the senses (sight, taste, touch, hearing, smell).

5. **Sentence fluency and conventions.** Copy the sentence that begins, "In the center of the . . . " Underline the appositive in this sentence.

**Your Turn to Write:
Describe a Place**

Now you'll write your own descriptive essay about a specific place. Read the assignment carefully and follow the strategies and instructions for each stage of the writing process.

## Assignment

Your school's fund-raising committee is creating a recipe book called *Teenage Comfort Food*. The book will include two types of writing: descriptions of students' favorite places to eat and students' favorite recipes. The book will be sold to school families.

For the book, write an essay that describes your favorite place to eat. This place could be a fine restaurant, your grandmother's kitchen, the bleachers at a baseball game, or some other place. For your reader, create a mental picture of the place by describing sights, sounds, smells, tastes, and textures. Your essay should be approximately 400 words long.

Prewrite

**Analyze the Prompt.** The following questions will help you identify important details in the writing assignment. Write your answers on separate paper.

1. What is the purpose of this essay?
2. Who is the audience for this essay?
3. How long does the essay need to be?

**Choose a Topic.** On your paper, list three different places where you enjoy eating. Now, in your mind, take a look around each place. Notice the sights, smells, and sounds that you find there. Which of these places would you most enjoy telling a friend about? Circle the name of this place. This is the subject of your essay.

**Gather Ideas and Details.** Use the following table to list sensory details about the place you chose to write about. Some details have been filled in as examples.

**Sensory Details About** _____ (the name of the place)

| sight | sound | taste | touch | smell |
|-------|-------|-------|-------|-------|
| green countertops | creaking floor | buttery cinnamon rolls | warmth of the room | baking bread |
|  |  |  |  |  |

**Organize Ideas and Details.** Now it is time to plan the arrangement of ideas and details in your descriptive essay. Here are three methods of organization that may work in your description:

- **Order of importance.** Include details from most to least important. Start with the most noticeable detail about this place. Move on to the detail that you notice next, and so on in order to build a complete picture.

- **Time order.** Include details in the order in which you notice them as you enter this place and look around.

- **Spatial order.** Describe the place from top to bottom or left to right. Begin with the eye-catching mural next to the entryway, for example, and move clockwise around the room from there.

The following model shows part of an outline for a descriptive essay. First, the writer introduces her subject: Grandmother's kitchen. Then she describes her first impressions as she enters the room. Next, she describes what she notices after that. She uses time order, or order of experience, as her method of organization.

I. Introduction
    A. Fine restaurants not my favorites
    B. Plain room in old farmhouse
    C. Grandmother's kitchen
II. First impressions
    A. Smell of baking bread
    B. Buttermilk biscuits
    C. Yeast bread
    D. Cinnamon rolls
III. Second impressions
    A. Washing machine
    B. Green countertops
    C. Stove

Which method of organization would work best for your essay—order of importance, time order, or spatial arrangement? Choose one of these methods.

**Organize Your Description.** At the top of a sheet of paper, write the name of your place and the method of organization that you chose. Then use a numbered list or outline format to plan the structure of your essay.

 Draft

Now it's time to write the first draft of your descriptive essay. As you know, three ingredients of a strong essay are the introduction, the body, and the conclusion.

**Introduction.** A strong essay begins with an introduction that catches the reader's interest and states the topic of the essay. In your descriptive essay, you should identify your place and give readers an idea, image, or detail that will make them want to know more.

Here are a few strategies for catching your reader's interest.

- Give interesting facts or figures.

  In a city of more than 150 fine restaurants, one stands out above the rest: the Riverboat.

- Include one or more sensory details that will spark your reader's imagination.

  The scent of Mexican herbs and spices wafts toward you. Savory cumin blends with the sharper scents of cilantro and onion.

- Give an unexpected fact about the place that will make your reader want to know more.

  This honor was earned long ago by a plain room in an old farmhouse.

**Write Your Introduction.** Write an introductory paragraph for your essay. Be sure to
- introduce your place by name
- give your readers an idea, image, or detail that will make them want to know more about this place

**Body paragraphs.** The body of a descriptive essay is the middle part, the part that comes after the introduction and before the conclusion. This is the heart of your description. Here, you should describe your place in a way that makes readers feel as though they are right there. Following a clear method of organization and using sensory details will help you write strong body paragraphs.

**Write the Body Paragraphs of Your Essay.** Write the paragraphs that form the body of your descriptive essay. As you write, be sure to

- review the ideas and details you gathered during prewriting
- follow the outline you wrote
- use a consistent point of view

**Conclusion.** Your essay's conclusion brings your description of the place to an end. A strong conclusion adds something new to the image of the place while giving the sense that the description is now complete. Here is the conclusion to the essay about Grandmother's kitchen.

It may not be fancy, and it may not be modern, but Grandmother's kitchen is homey, full of love, and full of good memories. This room's delicious aromas and familiar layout mean "home" to me. In my heart, it has earned the honor of favorite place to eat.

**Write Your Conclusion.** Write a paragraph that will bring your descriptive essay to a satisfying close.

Revise

Have you ever picked up your cell to call a friend and then froze? The conversation is just too important to mess up. In your mind, you practice saying what you want to say. And then you practice it again, changing a few key words. Finally, when you've got the words just right, you dial the number.

In the same way, going over your written work gives you a chance to make it stronger. You can look at what you wrote and ask, "Is this exactly what I wanted to say? Is there a way that I can say it more clearly or in a more interesting way? These are questions that you answer during the revision stage of your writing process.

One way to make your writing stronger is with sentence variety. Sentence variety means that the essay has a mix of sentence types, sentence lengths, and sentence structures. The mini-lesson below explains how to add sentence variety by using appositives.

# Mini-Lesson: Using Appositives

If you've ever introduced a friend to your parents, then you have probably used an appositive. Try filling in these sentences with names of people you know.

This is my best friend, _____.

One of my friends, _____, is staying for dinner tonight.

In each of the examples above, the name you wrote on the blank line works as an *appositive* in the sentence.

→ An **appositive** is a word or phrase that identifies or re-names a noun or pronoun.

Appositives help to clarify key nouns by giving additional information. Here's another example:

My new neighbor, Victor Griego, owns a deli.
              appositive

In this example, the words *Victor Griego* give more information about the neighbor. This appositive gives the neighbor's name. Notice that a comma comes before and after the words *Victor Griego*.

→ Use **commas** to set off an appositive from the rest of the sentence.

Using appositives helps you to add variety to the sentence structures in your essay. Compare the following sentences.

| Two simple sentences | One sentence with an appositive |
|---|---|
| My favorite restaurant specializes in fine Mexican food. The restaurant's name is La Canasta. | My favorite restaurant, <u>La Canasta</u>, specializes in fine Mexican food. |
| My grandmother's house is an old farmhouse. It is my favorite place. | My grandmother's house, <u>an old farmhouse</u>, is my favorite place. |
| My grandmother is raising me. My grandmother is a woman in her sixties. | My grandmother, <u>a woman in her sixties</u>, is raising me. |

## Give It a Try: Revise Sentences to Add Appositives

On separate paper, rewrite each pair of simple sentences to form one sentence with an appositive.

1. The restaurant manager is my uncle. His name is Paul Hillson.

2. I eagerly tasted the entrée. It was a beef and cheese lasagna.

3. The mouthwatering aroma of my favorite food fills the air. My favorite food is hot dogs.

4. This symbol means that the dish is a healthy choice. This symbol is a tiny red heart.

5. New owners gave the building new life as a pizza parlor. The building was an old fire station.

## Give It a Try: Write a Sentence with an Appositive

Read through your descriptive essay, examining sentences in which you introduce people, places, or things. Revise one of these sentences to include an appositive.

**Revise Your Descriptive Essay.** By rewriting a sentence to include an appositive, you have already begun revising your essay. To continue, use the checklist below to evaluate your work. The Descriptive Essay Rubric that follows the checklist will help you determine how strong your paragraph is and where to make changes.

### Ideas
❑ Read the sentence(s) where you introduce the place. Place a check mark next to it if it catches your reader's attention. If not, revise it to make it more interesting.
❑ Underline three details that help to describe your place.

### Organization
❑ Check that the descriptive details are arranged in a logical order. Revise or move any that are out of place.

### Voice
❑ Find three words that show your attitude or opinion about this place. Write *voice* above them.
❑ What point of view did you use, first, second, or third person? Check that it is used consistently.

### Word choice
❑ Circle three specific and expressive words you used to describe this place.
❑ Write *sensory det.* above two sensory details you used. Add more if necessary.

### Sentence fluency
❑ Have you used a variety of sentence structures? Revise some sentences if necessary.

# Descriptive Essay Rubric

| | 4<br>Strong | 3<br>Effective | 2<br>Developing | 1<br>Beginning |
|---|---|---|---|---|
| **Ideas** | One place is described. Each detail clearly relates. | The subject is clear, but some details do not relate. | The writer is beginning to make the subject clear. | The subject is not clear. Most details do not relate. |
| **organization** | Descriptive details are arranged logically. | Most details are arranged logically. | Organization of details is awkward. | Details are in random order. |
| **voice** | The writing style is distinctive and helps the reader connect to the description. | The writing style draws the reader in to the description but doesn't have a personal flair. | The writing style of one or two sentences, but not all, draws in the reader. | Writing is mechanical, making it hard for readers to connect to the description. |
| **word choice** | Specific and lively words are used. Sensory details are used with skill. | Many words are specific and lively. Many sensory details are included. | Words are simple but mostly correct. A few sensory details are used. | Vocabulary is limited. Sensory details are not present or not clear. |
| **sentence fluency** | Sentence variety creates a pleasing rhythm. | Sentences are varied in structure, but some are awkward. | Sentences are complete but are mostly short and simple. | Sentences are mostly of one type or are incomplete. |
| **conventions** | Capitalization, spelling, punctuation, and grammar are correct. | There are few errors in capitalization, spelling, punctuation, and grammar. | There are many errors in capitalization, spelling, punctuation, and grammar. | Errors in conventions make it hard to understand the writing. |

## Edit

How is editing your writing different from revising it?

When you revise your essay, you make changes to strengthen ideas, organization, word choice, sentences, and voice. The changes at this stage can be large or small. For example, you may combine two sentences or add two new details.

During the editing stage, you look for mistakes in spelling, punctuation, capitalization, and grammar (the conventions of writing), and you fix them. These edits are usually small. You add a comma, for instance, or capitalize a name. These edits may be small, but they are important. The conventions of writing are road signs that keep your reader moving in the right direction. Leave one out, or put in the wrong sign, and the reader could veer right off the road.

**Edit Your Descriptive Essay.** Edit the revised copy of your descriptive essay. The following questions will help you decide what to change, remove, or leave in place.

### Conventions
- ❑ Did you capitalize proper nouns, such as the names of places and people?
- ❑ Did you use a comma after each introductory word, phrase, or clause?
- ❑ Did you use a comma when you joined sentences with a coordinating conjunction?
- ❑ Did you correct spelling mistakes, either with a friend's help or by using a dictionary?
- ❑ Did you correct grammar mistakes, either with a friend's help or by using a grammar handbook?

**PUBLISH**

**Presentation.** Prepare your descriptive essay for publication by neatly writing or typing the final, edited copy.

**Publish Your Paragraph.** Here are some ways to publish your descriptive essay.

- ❏ Give a copy to friends or family members who have eaten with you in the place you described.
- ❏ With classmates, create a Web site that showcases your favorite things. Include your essay under the heading *Favorite Places to Eat*.
- ❏ Visit your place with a camera and capture images that illustrate your written description. Post the photos on your Web site (see the checklist item above), or use the photos and written description to create a personal memento.

## Evaluate Your Essay

Your teacher will either assess your essay, ask you to self-assess your essay, or ask you to switch with a partner and assess each other's work.

## Evaluate the Model Essay

Work with a partner to evaluate the following descriptive essay. Use the rubric on page 31 and write your score here: _____. In a class discussion, explain the score that you gave.

## Grandmother's Kitchen

On special occasions, I have eaten at several fine restaurants in town. Each experience was memorable. However, none was special enough to earn the honor of being my favorite place to eat. This honor was earned long ago by a plain room in an old farmhouse. Where is it? This place is my Grandmother's kitchen, a room filled with delicious smells, functional appliances, and the comfort of home.

When I enter the kitchen, the first thing I notice is usually the smell of baking bread. Most mornings, Grandmother whips up a batch of buttermilk biscuits. Sometimes she serves them with butter and jam, with eggs on the side. Sometimes she splits them open and smothers them in creamy sausage gravy. If there is a biscuit left over, she'll use it to make me a ham sandwich for my school lunch. But biscuits aren't the only bread that fill this kitchen with a mouthwatering smell. Grandmother also bakes fluffy white yeast bread on the weekends, and sometimes she makes buttery cinnamon rolls studded with fat raisins.

As I sit to eat at a small square wooden table, I let my gaze wander around the room. To my left, next to the doorway, is the clothes washing machine. Grandmother makes this hulky appliance double as counter space. She throws a tablecloth over it and sets bowls of food or stacks of dishes there just before a meal. A green countertop runs along the rest of the wall, with the white stove set right at the center point. All the mixing and baking magic happen here.

At right angles to this counter is a narrow window in the north wall of the room. Bright light floods in through sparkling windowpanes and handmade white curtains. To the right of it is a counter with a wide old porcelain sink set in it. Above and below, shelves hold plates, bowls, and glasses. The space is finished out on the east wall with a pantry, the refrigerator, and the clothes dryer. On cold winter days, we make sure to wash a load of clothes because the dryer helps to keep this old room warm.

It may not be fancy, and it may not be modern, but Grandmother's kitchen is homey, full of love, and full of good memories. This room's delicious aromas and familiar layout mean "home" to me. In my heart, it has earned the honor of favorite place to eat.

# Describe a Scientific Subject

As a writer, you can use descriptive writing for many different purposes. You can use descriptions to make stories and poems more vivid, and you can use descriptions to make explanations clearer. Scientists use descriptive writing to help make scientific facts and ideas clear. They use descriptive writing to answer *how* and *why* questions such as, *How does a clock work? Why is it easier to climb a hill on a path that zigzags than on a path that goes straight up?*

In this chapter, you will examine scientific facts about simple machines, and you'll write a description of one type of simple machine. In doing so, you will build on your skills of descriptive writing and practice using scientific terms. In addition, you'll continue learning about the traits of writing, described in the table below.

## Six Traits of **Describing a Scientific Subject**

| | |
|---|---|
| Ideas | The purpose of the description is clear. Each idea and detail helps to accomplish this purpose |
| organization | The article contains a beginning, a middle, and an end. The ideas and details are arranged logically. |
| voice | The writer uses an objective, fact-focused tone. The writer shines through as a trustworthy source of the information. |
| word choice | Scientific words and terms make the description precise. |
| sentence fluency | The writer uses a variety of sentence types and structures. Transition words and phrases link ideas clearly. |
| conventions | Capitalization, spelling, punctuation, and grammar are correct. |

In the following description, the writer uses scientific words and terms to describe the use of a simple machine.

Levers can help people lift loads far heavier than they could manage without this simple machine. For instance, imagine one ten-year-old child trying to lift another 10-year-old child two feet up into the air. She could not do it--not without a lever, that is.

Now imagine a seesaw: a board balanced on a post. One child sits on one end, and another child sits on the other end. As the first child lets her weight press down, the board pivots on the fulcrum (the balancing point). In this way, she creates a force that lifts the load (the other child) at the opposite end of the board. A simple tool has made a seemingly impossible task possible.

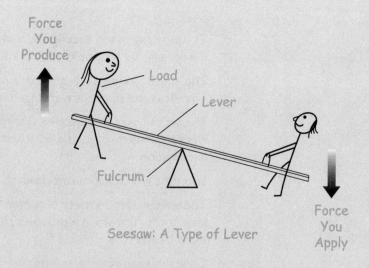

Seesaw: A Type of Lever

# Give It a Try: Examine the Model Passage

With your teacher's permission, work with a partner to answer the following questions. Refer to the model passage on the previous page, and write your answers on separate paper.

1. **Ideas and organization.**
   a. What is the main subject of this description?
   b. What is the main idea of the first paragraph?
   c. What is the main idea of the second paragraph?
2. **Word choice.** List two words that are examples of scientific vocabulary.
3. **Voice.** Copy one statement of fact from the passage.
4. **Sentence fluency.** List two transition words or phrases from the passage.
5. **Conventions.** Why does the writer place some words inside parentheses?

Your Turn to Write:
Describe a Scientific Subject

Now you'll write your own scientific description. Read the assignment carefully and follow the strategies and instructions for each stage of the writing process.

## Assignment

*You and Your World*, a science magazine, is publishing a special issue on simple machines. Topics will include the lever, the inclined plane, the wedge, the wheel and axle, the screw, and the pulley.

Writers are invited to submit a 200-word article that describes a simple machine in action. Articles should be written for students in grades 6–12, and they must include a sketch of the simple machine.

Choose one of the topics listed above, and write a descriptive article for *You and Your World*. Follow the guidelines above.

**Prewrite**

**Analyze the Prompt.** Use the writing assignment to answer the following questions. Write your answers on separate paper.

1. What is the purpose of this article?

2. Who is the audience for this article?

3. How long does the article need to be?

**Choose a Topic.** Complete the steps below to learn about simple machines and choose one as your subject for writing.

1. Choose one type of simple machine and find out more about it. Write a few sentences that
   - tell what kind of work the simple machine does
   - name an example of this kind of simple machine

2. Gather with a small group of classmates who learned about the same simple machine as you did. Compare your findings.

3. In a class discussion, teach the class about your simple machine.

4. Based on the class discussion, select the simple machine you would like to write about. Write its name here:

_____

**Gather Ideas and Details.** When it comes to the simple machine you chose to describe, what do you know already? What do you need to find out? On a blank sheet of paper, create a 3Ws table like the one on the next page. Use it to organize your knowledge, questions, and findings.

**My writing topic** _____

| What I Know | What I Need to Find Out | What I Found Out |
|---|---|---|
| your details here | your details here | your details here |
| | | |

**Organize Ideas and Details.** Use an outline or a list format to plan the arrangement of ideas and details in your description. Here is an example of how one writer organized ideas and details for an article about the pulley. He used an informal outline and planned the parts of his article using the words *First*, *Second*, and so on.

First, I will explain what a pulley is.
- A type of simple machine
- Grooved wheel and rope
- Used to pull something up or down

Second, I will identify an example of a pulley, a flagpole.

Third, I will describe how a flagpole works.
- Example of a pulley on a flag
- Show diagram of flagpole.

Fourth, I will tell why the flagpole works.
- Details about where you hook the flag and how you pull the rope.
- Helps you conquer heights!

> **T!p**
>
> As you outline your article, you may notice that you need additional supporting details. Create another 3W's table like the one above. Then go back and observe your subject and collect the additional details you need.

Draft

One of the traits of good scientific writing is using scientific language. **Scientific language** is the special vocabulary used to express science-related facts and ideas. For instance, *igneous rock* is a scientific term for a particular kind of *rock*. *Metamorphosis* is a scientific term for *change*. Compare the following definitions.

> **change** The act of becoming different.

> **metamorphosis** A developmental change in the form or structure of an animal after birth or hatching.

In a general conversation, using the word *change* is good enough. But if you are writing a scientific article to describe the change of a caterpillar into a butterfly, then the scientific term *metamorphosis* allows you to be as accurate as possible.

**Write Your Scientific Article.** Write the first draft of your article about a simple machine. As you write, use scientific language to express ideas as accurately as possible. The following word bank contains some scientific words and terms that you might use, depending on your topic. As you write, add new words to the box.

| Scientific Language Word Bank | | | |
| --- | --- | --- | --- |
| simple machine | force | resistance | magnify |
| pivot | incline | effort | acceleration |
| fulcrum | magnify | | |

*Additional Science Vocabulary:*

## Revise

One of the tricks to great organization in writing is to use transitions to link ideas. Transitions can show cause and effect, sequence, order of importance, and much more. The following mini-lesson explains how you can use transitions to show the connections between ideas in your writing.

## Mini-Lesson: Using Transition Words and Phrases

One of the easiest things to leave out of a rough draft is transitions. Why? Because when you write, you already know how your ideas connect. They're *your* ideas, after all. However, you are writing for an audience, not just yourself. Your audience will not automatically know how your ideas connect. Therefore, you must show the connections by using *transitions*.

→ **Transitions** are words or phrases that connect one idea to another, one sentence to another, or one paragraph to another.

### Transition Words and Phrases

**To Show Location**

| | | | |
|---|---|---|---|
| above | beneath | in front of | on top of |
| ahead | between | inside | outside |
| behind | beyond | near | throughout |
| below | before | next to | under |

**To Show Time**

| after | finally | later | until |
|---|---|---|---|
| at last | first, second, etc. | meanwhile | soon |
| before | in the past | next | then |
| during | last | now | following |

**To Add**

| also | as well | finally | furthermore |
|---|---|---|---|
| and | besides | for example | in addition |
| another | besides that | for instance | moreover |

**To Show Importance or Order of Importance**

| even greater | first, second, etc. | most significantly |
|---|---|---|
| finally | most important | next |

**To Show Comparison or Contrast**

| although | however | likewise | otherwise |
|---|---|---|---|
| but | in contrast | nevertheless | similarly |
| even though | like | on the other hand | yet |

**To Show Cause or Effect**

| as a result | consequently | since | therefore |
|---|---|---|---|
| because | for this reason | so | |

In the following paragraph from an article on the pulley, the writer has added transition words and phrases to show important connections between ideas.

The pulley helps you raise the flag. *First,* Hook the flag to one side of the rope circle. (Use the hooks that are there.) *Then,* Pull down on the other side of the rope circle. *As you pull down on one side,* The flag on the other side goes higher and higher. Pull until the flag goes up to the top of the flagpole. *Finally,* Wrap the rope around the cleat on the flagpole to hold it in place.

# Give It a Try: Use Transitions in Your Writing

Check your descriptive article for places where ideas, sentences, or paragraphs connect. Revise the draft by adding transitions to make these connections clear.

**Revise Your Scientific Description.** Use the following checklist to revise the rough draft of your descriptive article. The Descriptive Article Rubric that follows the checklist will help you determine how strong your article is and where to make revisions.

### Ideas
- ❑ Check that your introduction makes your purpose for writing clear. If not, rewrite it.
- ❑ Underline three details that help to accomplish the purpose of your article. Cross out any irrelevant details.

### Organization
- ❑ Be sure your article has a beginning, a middle, and an end.
- ❑ Did you arrange ideas and details in a logical order? Rearrange details if necessary.

### Voice
- ❑ Find words that show your objective, factual tone. Write *voice* above them. Revise words that are not objective.
- ❑ As the writer, do you shine through as an authority on your subject?

**Word choice**

❏ Do you use scientific language where it is appropriate for your audience? Circle three examples.

**Sentence fluency**

❏ Do you use transitions to link ideas and help sentences flow smoothly? Circle three examples.

# Descriptive Article Rubric

|  | 4 Strong | 3 Effective | 2 Developing | 1 Beginning |
|---|---|---|---|---|
| Ideas | The writer describes a simple machine and clearly describes how it works. | The writer identifies a simple machine and describes how it works. | The writer identifies a simple machine and one or two details about how it works. | The writer names a simple machine but does not describe how it works. |
| organization | The article has a beginning, a middle, and an end. | The article has a beginning and a middle, but the end is weak. | The article does not have a beginning or an end. | The article includes descriptions in random order. |
| voice | The writer uses an objective tone. | The writer uses an objective tone in some paragraphs. | The writer uses an objective tone in some sentences. | The writer's tone is not objective. |
| word choice | The writer uses scientific language. | The writer uses some scientific language. | The writer uses a scientific word or term. | The writer does not use scientific language. |
| sentence fluency | Sentences are varied. Transitions connect ideas, sentences, and paragraphs. | Sentences are varied. Transitions connect some ideas and sentences. | One or two sentences add variety. One or two transitions are used. | Sentences all sound alike (no variety). Transitions are absent. |
| conventions | Titles are written correctly. Few errors in spelling or grammar are present. | Titles are written correctly. Several errors in spelling or grammar are present. | Many errors in titles, spelling, or grammar are present. | Errors in conventions make it difficult to understand the article. |

## Edit

As you know, editing your article means finding and correcting errors in capitalization, spelling, punctuation, and grammar. As you grow as a writer, you will develop your own system for identifying and fixing these kinds of errors. What system do you currently use? How could you make your system even more effective?

**Share and Edit.** In a class discussion, share your personal tips and techniques for identifying and correcting errors in one or more of these categories:

**Conventions**
- Capitalization
- Spelling
- Punctuation
- Grammar

Then use ideas from the class discussion to edit your article.

**Presentation.** Prepare your scientific article for publication by neatly writing or typing the final, edited copy.

## PUBLISH

**Publish Your Article.** Here are some ideas for publishing your scientific article.

❑ Share your article with a younger student who is learning about simple machines.

❑ Create a demonstration video to show a simple machine at work. Include a voice-over of yourself reading your descriptive article aloud.

❑ Work with classmates to create your own issue of *You and Your World* magazine. Create a magazine cover and a table of contents to go along with your articles and diagrams. Make copies for each person who is published in the magazine—and make extra copies to pass out to friends.

## Evaluate Your Article

Your teacher will either assess your article, ask you to self-assess your article, or ask you to switch with a partner and assess each other's work.

## Evaluate the Model Article

Work with a partner to evaluate the following scientific article. Use the rubric on page 46 and write your score here: _____. In a class discussion, explain the score you gave.

A Simple Machine Helps Us Conquer Heights

A pulley is a type of simple machine. It uses a grooved wheel and a rope, which fits into the groove. We use pulleys to pull a load up or to lower a load down. We can also use a pulley to move a load from side to side. Let's study the pulley on a flagpole.

A flagpole is really tall. How can you get the flag from ground level all the way to the top of the pole? You use a pulley. On a flagpole, the pulley is at the top of the pole. The rope runs up the flagpole, through the pulley, and back down the flagpole. The ends of the rope are tied together, like a circle. Look at this diagram of a flagpole.

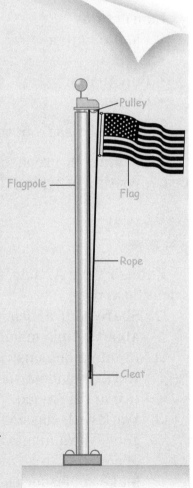

The pulley helps you raise the flag. First, hook the flag to one side of the rope circle. (Use the hooks that are there.) Then pull down on the other side of the rope circle. As you pull down on one side, the flag on the other side goes higher and higher. Pull until the flag goes up to the top of the flagpole. Finally, wrap the rope around the cleat on the flagpole to hold it in place.

Simple machines like the pulley help us conquer heights!

# Test Writing:
# The Descriptive Essay

You have probably written short or long responses on tests. Take a moment to list a few kinds of writing you have done on tests for different classes

Why do teachers ask you to give written responses on tests? They may want to see if you can remember and describe what you learned. For instance, a science teacher may ask you to describe the parts of a cell. A history teacher may ask you to describe a pioneer town.

In English class, teachers ask you to write test essays to see if you can generate ideas and write with careful consideration for the traits of writing. In this chapter, you'll learn more about the process of writing a descriptive essay for a test.

## Six Traits of a Descriptive Test Essay

| | |
|---|---|
| Ideas | The writer has written about the topic stated in the writing prompt. Each detail clearly relates to this topic. |
| organization | The essay has a beginning, a middle, and an end. Ideas and details are arranged logically. |
| voice | The writing style fits with the purpose and audience of the description. |
| word choice | The writer uses specific and lively words and sensory details. |
| sentence fluency | The writer uses a variety of sentence types and structures. |
| conventions | Capitalization, spelling, punctuation, and grammar are correct. |

## Preparing to Write Your Test Essay

During your time in school, you will see essay prompts that are written and arranged in different ways. A prompt may be short and to the point, or it may include a list of tips or reminders. The prompt may be set in a box or typed across the top of a page. Here is an example of a prompt for a descriptive composition.

---

**Instructions**
You have 25 minutes to complete the written composition. Read the prompt below. Then use separate paper to plan and draft your composition. Only your draft will be scored.

**Writing Prompt**
At one time or another, most people plan a party for friends. Before the guests arrive, the host decorates the room, arranges furniture, sets out food and drinks, and makes other party arrangements. If you were planning a party for your friends, what would the room look like just before they arrived? What scents would be in the air? What tastes would be waiting for the guests? Write an essay in which you describe your ideal party, just before it begins. Use sensory details and vivid words so that your readers can picture it clearly.

---

### 1. Study the Prompt
Before you begin to write your essay, take a few moments to study the prompt. Answer these important questions:

**What is the purpose of the essay?** Scan the prompt for key words that tell you what kind of essay to write.

**Words That Signal a Descriptive Essay**

| | |
|---|---|
| describe | description |
| sensory details | picture/mental picture |

**What should you write about?** Study the prompt to determine exactly what you must write. Look for an *imperative sentence*: one that gives a command or makes a request. In the prompt on page 50, the imperative sentence is this one:

*Write an essay in which you describe your ideal party, just before it begins.*

This sentence is your assignment in a nutshell. It tells you exactly what to write. If you are allowed to mark on the test document, underline this sentence to help you focus on it.

Other sentences in the prompt make the topic clear and remind you how to stay on track. For instance, read this sentence from the prompt:

*Use sensory details and vivid words so that your readers can picture it clearly.*

This sentence comes just after the imperative sentence and reminds you that a strong description includes sensory details and vivid words. Be sure to follow these reminders.

**How much time do you have to write?** The sample prompt states that you have 25 minutes to complete the assignment. If a prompt does not state a time limit, this information may be printed on another page in the test booklet, or your teacher may post the information in your classroom.

## 2. Plan Your Time

After studying the prompt, make a quick plan for how to use your time. If you have 25 minutes in which to write the test, you could use your time as follows:

5–7 minutes:     Study the prompt and complete the prewriting.

13–15 minutes: Write the essay.

5 minutes:       Revise and edit the essay.

**TOOLKIT**

For a descriptive essay, useful strategies include
- a descriptive details table (like the one in Chapter 1)
- a sensory details table (like the one in Chapter 2)

## 3. Prewrite

During the time set aside for prewriting, you should gather ideas and details for your topic and organize the information.

**Gather ideas and details.** Use a few of your prewriting minutes to gather ideas and details. Choose a method that works for you.

In the following model, the writer gathers ideas and details for an essay that describes his ideal party.

### Sensory Details About My Ideal Party

| sight | sound | taste | touch | smell |
|---|---|---|---|---|
| baloons and streamers everywhere; small treat bags for everyone | all my friends' favorite songs playing in the background, or our favorite radio station | bite-size food on platters: pizza bites, nachos, chocolate-dipped strawberries, lots of chocolate and vanilla cupcakes | a gross-out game of "feel the eyeballs" | the smell of just-delivered pizza |

**T!p** The model above uses completely written words, but you can save time by using abbreviations in your prewriting. Just remember to spell out words fully when you write the essay to be graded.

**Organize the information.** Use your remaining prewriting time to plan the arrangement of information in your essay. During a 25-minute testing period, it is reasonable to plan for a 3–5 paragraph essay. Don't try to create a formal or complicated outline. Instead, jot down key points to include in the introduction, body, and conclusion.

<u>beginning</u>
--reason for party: winter break
--where: my living room

<u>middle</u>
(use spatial arrangement of details)
--paragraph 1: coffee table filled with food
      smells, tastes
--paragraph 2: sounds
      music
--paragraph 3: games and treats that are waiting

<u>end</u>
--This will be an ideal party because it appeals to each of my guests' senses.

## Writing Your Essay

Now that you have studied the prompt and planned the essay's content, you can begin writing. To help yourself write quickly and purposefully, stick to the plan you made during prewriting. Refer to it between paragraphs to keep yourself on track.

Often, the hardest sentence to write is the first sentence. Once you get that written, other ideas follow more easily. To get that first sentence written quickly, use ideas from the writing prompt. For example, the writing prompt on page 50 asks you to write about your "ideal party." Use these key words in your first sentence, as in the model paragraph below.

**Word choice:** The writer uses key words from the writing prompt.

My ideal party would be on the Friday afternoon that school lets out before winter break. This is reason enough to celebrate, and the sight of my party would put everyone in the mood for fun. The event would take place at my home in my living room, and it would be a treat for the senses.

**Voice:** The first-person point of view lets the writer's voice shine through. The prompt asks specifically about your ideal party.

## Polishing Your Test Essay

Your reader will expect you to review your essay to correct mistakes in capitalization, spelling, punctuation, and grammar.

Writing a test essay is different from preparing an essay outside of class. For a timed test, you don't have time to mark up a draft and then write a clean, revised copy. Instead, make your corrections directly on the copy to be scored. Using editing marks can help you revise and polish your essay quickly. Make all marks as neatly and cleanly as possible.

The table on the next page explains commonly used editing marks. Below that, you'll see how the writer of the model essay uses editing marks to add a comma, create a complex sentence, add an appositive, and make *people* possessive.

| | |
|---|---|
| = | capitalize a letter. |
| / | Change a Capital letter to lowercase. |
| e | Delete a word word or lettter. |
| ^ | Insert a leter word here. |
| ^ | Insert a comma here. |
| ¶ | ¶Start a new paragraph. |
| ∩ | switch teh order of |

When the guests walk in the door the first thing
they will see is the coffee table in front of the sofa.
It will be covered with platters of bite-size food.
Nachos will drip with melting, golden cheese. A
freshly delivered pizza will fill the air with the scent
of garlic and pepperoni. It will be cut into small
squares for easy eating. A tray of chocolate-
covered strawberries will tempt people sweet tooth.
Even more than that, two kinds of cupcakes will
tempt people.

# Evaluating a Descriptive Test Essay

Teachers understand that you have a limited time to plan, write, and polish your test essay. They are not expecting the essay to be perfect. Despite the time limit, teachers do expect you to

- show your ability to write to the prompt
- include relevant details in an organized manner
- show careful consideration for the conventions of capitalization, spelling, punctuation, and grammar

The following rubric shows guidelines for evaluating a descriptive test essay.

# Descriptive Test Essay Rubric

| | 4 Strong | 3 Effective | 2 Developing | 1 Beginning |
|---|---|---|---|---|
| **Ideas** | The writer wrote to the prompt. Each detail clearly relates. | The writer wrote to the prompt, but a few details do not relate. | The writer included some details relating to the prompt. | The writer did not write to the prompt. |
| **organization** | Information is arranged logically. | Most information is arranged logically. | Organization of information is awkward. | Information is included in random order. |
| **voice** | The writing style helps the reader connect to the description. | The writing style of some paragraphs draws the reader in. | The writing style of one or two sentences draws the reader in. | Writing is mechanical, making it hard for readers to connect. |
| **word choice** | Vivid words and sensory details are used. | A few vivid words and sensory details are used. | One or two vivid words or sensory details are used. | No vivid words or sensory details are used. |
| **sentence fluency** | A variety of sentence types is used in a pleasing rhythm. | A variety of sentence types is used, but some may be awkward. | Sentences are complete but are mostly short and simple. | Sentences are mostly of one type or are incomplete. |
| **conventions** | Few errors in capitalization, spelling, punctuation, or grammar are present. | Several errors in capitalization, spelling, punctuation, or grammar are present. | Errors in capitalization, spelling, punctuation, and grammar do not prevent understanding. | Errors in capitalization, spelling, punctuation, and grammar prevent understanding. |

# Evaluate a Model Test Essay

Work with a partner to evaluate the following model composition. Use the rubric on page 57 and write your score here: _____. In a class discussion, explain the score you gave.

### A Sense-sational party

My ideal party would be on the Friday afternoon that school lets out before winter break. This is reason enough to celebrate, and the sight of my party would put everyone in the mood for fun. The event would take place at my home in my living room, and it would be a treat for the senses.

When the guests walk in the door the first thing they will see is the coffee table in front of the sofa. It will be covered with platters of bite-size food. Nachos will drip with melting, golden cheese. A freshly delivered pizza will fill the air with the scent of garlic and pepperoni. It will be cut into small squares for easy eating. A tray of chocolate-covered strawberries will tempt people sweet tooth. Even more than that, two kinds of cupcakes will tempt people.

Once guests drool over the food, they will begin to notice the music playing in the background, not too loud and not too soft. Each guest will notice that I have included at least one of his or her favorite songs.

After that, guests will walk around the room. They will eat. They'll notice that there are treat bags sitting everywhere. These will be colored paper bags decorated with ribbons and labeled with guests names. Each guest will find a bag full of fun stuff to take home. There will also be "Gross Sensation Stations" where people can stick their hands in a bowl of "eyeballs" (peeled grapes) or "guts" (fat, buttery pasta noodles) and things like that.

With the food, the smells, the perfectly chosen music, the brite party bags, and the gross-out games, the party will appeal to each of the five senses. It will be sense-sational!

Give your essay a title that will catch your reader's interest. Often, the best time to decide on a title is after you have written the essay. In the model, the writer uses a key word from the conclusion (*sense-sational*) to form the title. He is making a play on the words *sense* and *sensational*.

Practice what you have learned by completing the following task.

**Instructions**

You have 25 minutes to complete the written composition. Read the prompt below. Then use separate paper to plan and draft your composition. Only your draft will be scored.

**Writing Prompt**

Some people have their own private bedroom at home, and others don't. But nearly everyone likes to decorate and arrange personal space in his or her own way. If you could have your own room, large or small, how would you decorate and furnish it? What would it smell like in your room? What sounds would you hear in there? Write an essay in which you describe your ideal bedroom so that readers can picture it clearly.

# Descriptive Writing Wrap-Up

The activities and information in these pages will help you continue to strengthen your descriptive-writing skills. In You Be the Judge, use the Descriptive Writing Rubric to evaluate a student's work. The Ideas for Writing are additional descriptive-writing prompts you can use for practice. And finally, in the Unit 1 Reflections, you can list important ideas you have learned in this unit and set goals for future learning.

## You Be the Judge

Use what you've learned about the traits of descriptive writing to evaluate a student essay. First, review the traits of descriptive writing on page 2. Next, read the student essay printed below. Finally, in the rubric that follows the essay, assign the essay a score for each writing trait. In the space provided, explain each score that you assign.

### Brazilian Experience
#### Author Unknown

When I told my friends I was going to Brazil for three weeks, many questioned why I wanted to go. Some thought Brazil was all rainforest with few populous cities, others thought there was no cultural background to the country. Aside from the fact that I have an aunt in Belo Horizonte, I went to Brazil to experience a different culture and get away from the boredom of the suburbs. Brazil is a country full of life, from the lush botanical gardens in Rio de Janeiro to the very social people, to their favorite sport, soccer.

In Rio de Janeiro—one of Brazil's biggest cities—there is a botanical garden that covers over 100 acres. Calling it a garden is an understatement; it houses thousands of different plants and animals, all growing with little aid from humans. The exquisite gardens are very peaceful.

In the treetops, monkeys and tropical birds screech and hoot to one another. Some of the monkeys were so inquisitive, they followed me around and ate fruit from my hand.

Due to lush vegetation and flowers blooming almost all year round, butterflies and hummingbirds are everywhere. I was wearing a red shirt, and in no time the butterflies were all over me—I needed help to get them off.

The people of Brazil are some of the friendliest I've met. My aunt's friends welcomed me with such love and cheerfulness that I felt part of their family. We shared stories about our countries, and I played soccer until it was dinnertime.

When the food came, I was in heaven. We had a churrasco (barbeque) with everything from grilled chicken to filet mignon, pork and shish kebabs, and even chicken hearts, which sounded nauseating, but were so delicious, I ate five. After dinner, my new friends took me to a dance club where I met their friends. The next day they invited me to a professional soccer match.

Brazilians take their soccer very seriously, watching every game their team plays with so much enthusiasm and love that their bowls of chips have been known to fly into the air when their team scores. I went to a match in Belo Horizonte where the home team was playing their biggest rival. The stadium is the second largest in the world, and when all 100,000 people are screaming and shouting at once, it sounds more like a train than human beings. The stadium was so packed you could not even sit down. There were no real seats, anyway, just large concrete steps.

Whenever the home team was in a good position to score, insane chanting arose from the crowd. When the rival team scored, their little section went into an uproar with a series of unusually violent fights. When the home team finally won after a very close game, the whole stadium started to vibrate, with everyone jumping up and down and screaming. Afterwards, many people drove around the city honking their horns and waving flags until two in the morning. The Brazilians' love for soccer makes them fanatical about their teams and their country.

Going to Brazil was one of the best experiences I could possibly have. It is one of those countries which, once you visit, you never forget.

# Descriptive Writing Rubric

|  | 4<br>Strong | 3<br>Effective | 2<br>Developing | 1<br>Beginning |
|---|---|---|---|---|
| **Ideas**<br>Score_____ | *explanation:* | | | |
| **Organization**<br>Score_____ | *explanation:* | | | |
| **Voice**<br>Score_____ | *explanation:* | | | |
| **Word Choice**<br>Score_____ | *explanation:* | | | |
| **Sentence Fluency**<br>Score_____ | *explanation:* | | | |
| **Conventions**<br>Score_____ | *explanation:* | | | |

## Ideas for Writing

The assignments that follow will give you additional practice with descriptive writing. Your teacher may choose one or let you pick one that's most interesting to you.

1. The editor of your school newspaper has asked you to write an article for the entertainment section. She assigned you the theme of "imperfect yet beautiful." Choose one famous person and write an essay describing what makes this person imperfect

yet attractive. Use sensory details and vivid words to make your mental image come alive for readers.

2. If you and a good friend could take a day trip anyplace, where would it be? What would this place look like? Write a 300-word letter to a friend and describe a place that you would like to visit with him or her. Use sensory details and vivid words to help your friend feel as if he or she is right there in this place.

3. Your mayor is trying to raise awareness of the need to protect nature within the city. He has asked students to look around town at green spaces. Then he wants each student to write an essay describing what the city may have looked like 100 years ago *or* what it might look like 100 years in the future. At one of these time periods, how do you think green spaces help to form the city?

   Choose the past or the future, and write a 350-word essay in which you describe what you think your city and its green spaces would look like. Use sensory details to help your ideas come alive for your reader.

4. You have signed up as a tutor at an after-school math workshop. A teacher has assigned you to help younger students learn about one geometric shape. Possible topics include polygons and quadrilaterals. Write a paragraph of 150–200 words in which you describe *one* geometric shape using an example from real life. Use accurate mathematical terms to make your description precise.

# Unit 1 Reflections

How are you different as a writer now that you have completed this unit on descriptive writing? What new knowledge do you have? How is your writing stronger? What kinds of things could you work on to become even stronger as a descriptive writer? Use the following space to reflect on your work in this unit and to set goals for the future.

## Focus on Me: My Achievements as a Descriptive Writer

What I've learned about descriptive writing in this unit:

Ways my descriptive writing is stronger now:

Things I can do to practice my skills of descriptive writing:

# Expository Writing

## Get to Know the Genre: Expository Writing

Life is full of questions. *How do I fix a flat tire on my bicycle? Why is Walter Dean Myers your favorite author? What caused you to quit the basketball team?* To find answers to life's questions, you can read (or write) expository writing.

**Expository writing** makes a subject clear for readers through the use of examples and evidence. A clear thesis statement, solid supporting ideas, and a strong conclusion help to form a successful expository essay.

> You can write about *anything,* and if you write well enough, even the reader with no intrinsic [built-in] interest in the subject will become involved.
> —TRACY KIDDER *(American nonfiction writer, 1945–)*

## Give It a Try: Ask Questions

In the spaces below, spend five minutes listing questions that could be answered with different kinds of expository writing. A few questions are included to get you started.

| Expository Category | My Questions |
|---|---|
| **How-To** (tells how to do, build, or accomplish something) | How do I install extra shelves in my closet? |
| **Explanatory** (explains the reasons for an action or a viewpoint) | Why do I want to visit Alaska? |
| **Cause and Effect** (explains what caused something else to happen, or what the effects of an action are) | Why did the doghouse I built fall apart? How does "test stress" affect me? |

As with other forms of writing, a strong piece of expository writing includes specific traits. The following table explains traits of effective expository writing.

## Six Traits of **Expository Writing**

| Ideas | The topic is narrowed to a specific subject to be explained. Each detail clearly relates to the topic. |
|---|---|
| organization | Details are arranged with care, such as in order of importance, from general to specific, or order of steps in a sequence. |
| voice | The writing style fits with the purpose and audience of the explanation. |
| word choice | Specific nouns and verbs help the reader understand what the writer is explaining or how a process is completed. |
| sentence fluency | Declarative sentences are used to give information. A variety of sentence types and structures creates a pleasing rhythm to the writing. |
| conventions | Capitalization, spelling, punctuation, and grammar are correct. |

### Real-World Example

The following paragraph is taken from *Mark Twain Along the Mississippi*, a biography written by Wayne Youngblood. In this paragraph, Youngblood explains why he thinks Mark Twain, author of *Tom Sawyer* and other books, is such a beloved American.

**Ideas:** The topic sentence states the main idea of the paragraph.

**Word choice:** vivid word

**Sentence fluency:** This long sentence is followed by a shorter sentence.

**Ideas:** The writer explains his main idea by giving three supporting reasons (labeled 1–3 in the paragraph).

    In many ways, Mark Twain was an embodiment of quite a few of the best parts of the American spirit. ¹He was an adventurer and traveler, crisscrossing the United States and the globe throughout his lifetime, always looking for opportunities to explore new places. ²Twain was also a goodwill ambassador who easily connected with people from other cultures. Although he remained very much an American, he was comfortable socializing with, and living among, people in other countries. ³Mark Twain was a hard worker who never shirked his responsibilities. He never shied away from taking on a difficult job—even late in life when he was immensely popular—if he felt that it was the right thing to do.

**Voice:** The writer shows his good opinion of Mark Twain in the supporting details he chooses to include.

## Give It a Try: Examine the Model Paragraph

Can you find additional examples of the traits of writing in the model paragraph above? On separate paper, list three traits of writing. For each one, quote or describe an example from the model.

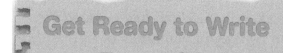

### Get Ready to Write

Now that you've explored the qualities of expository writing, you're ready to create some expositions of your own. In the chapters that follow, you'll write a how-to article about a fun project, an explanatory essay about the role of technology in your life, a cause-effect essay about a choice you've made, and an expository test essay about what courage means to you. You'll use the stages of the writing process—prewriting, drafting, revising, editing, and publishing—and you'll be presented with models and mini-lessons along the way.

As you work through these chapters, you can enrich your understanding by trying the suggestions below. These tips will help you connect what you're learning in this unit to your own life and the world around you.

---

### LEARNING TIPS

- As you go about daily life, notice the kinds of expository writing that help you through each day. Do you read user's manuals? Cereal boxes? Instructions for a new game? Think about the purpose of each example of expository writing. Does it tell how to do something? Does it explain an idea or viewpoint? Does it explain the cause or effects of an action or condition?

- Watch for expository writing in the reading you do for school. Think about how expository writing helps you understand ideas in math, science, and social studies.

- Practice your skills of explaining ideas in everyday life. Write an e-mail to someone simply to explain an opinion. In a conversation, explain to someone how to make something or perform a process. Use expository writing where it is appropriate in assignments for other classes.

- As you take part in sports or work on hobbies, think about how you could use expository writing to help someone else understand why you enjoy this activity.

# Chapter 5

# Write a How-To Article

In any given week, you are probably learning at least one new skill, sport, or hobby. Perhaps you are learning how to administer first aid, how to write using calligraphy, or how to organize a food drive for charity. Take a moment right now to think about things you are learning to do, or have recently learned how to do. On separate paper, list three of these things.

In this chapter, you will have the opportunity to explain how to do something that interests you. You might choose to write about something in the paragraph above, or you may want to choose a new topic. As with other forms of expository writing, your goal in writing a how-to article is to explain something clearly to your reader.

## Six Traits of How-To Article

| Ideas | The topic is narrowed to one specific goal to be accomplished. Each detail helps to explain a step in the process. |
|---|---|
| organization | The article explains the steps in a process in the order in which they must be completed. |
| voice | The writer uses a friendly, helpful tone. |
| word choice | Transition words make the order of steps clear. Specific nouns and verbs help the reader understand the process. |
| sentence fluency | Imperative sentences tell the reader what to do. Declarative sentences give information. |
| conventions | Capitalization, spelling, punctuation, and grammar are correct. |

In the how-to paragraph below, the author explains how to set the clock on a computer.

How to Set the Clock on a Computer

Setting the clock on a computer requires a few simple steps. First, turn on the computer and the monitor. Second, find the time readout on the desktop (the computer screen). Usually, it is displayed at the bottom left corner of the screen. Third, double-click the time. This action brings up a window called Date and Time Properties, or something similar. Fourth, in the Time box, type in the correct time. Make sure that the time zone is correct, too. Click on the Time Zone tab and select your time zone from the list. This way, when it is time to adjust for Daylight Saving Time, your computer will adjust at the proper time. Finally, click the Apply button, then the OK button. The window will close, and your computer's time is set.

## Give It a Try: Examine the Model Paragraph

Use the model paragraph above to answer the following questions. Write your answers on separate paper. Then, in a class discussion, explain your answers.

1. **Ideas.** What main goal does the article explain how to accomplish?
2. **Organization and word choice.** List three transition words that show the order of the steps in the process.

3. **Voice.** Does the writer mainly use the first-person point of view, the second-person point of view, or the third-person point of view? How do you know this?
4. **Sentence fluency.** Which type of sentence does the writer use most—declarative, imperative, or exclamatory?
5. **Conventions.** Identify two different rules of capitalization that the writer follows.

**Your Turn to Write: Compose a How-To Article**

Now you'll write your own informative how-to piece. Read the assignment carefully and follow the strategies and instructions for each stage of the writing process.

## Assignment

A new Web site for teens is adding a section called "Do It Yourself." This section will have how-to articles on topics in technology, crafts, cooking, daily living, and health and fitness. Write a 350–400-word article for the "Do It Yourself" page that explains how to do something, make something, or accomplish a goal. Be sure to use transitions to make the sequence of steps or actions clear.

**Prewrite**

**Analyze the Prompt.** Reread the assignment and answer the following questions. Write your answers on separate paper.
1. What is the purpose of this article?
2. Who is the audience for this article?
3. How long does the article need to be?

**Choose a Topic.** With your teacher's permission, gather in a small group and follow these steps.

1.  For five minutes, brainstorm for possible topics for a how-to article. Use the following table to organize your ideas. A few ideas are included to get you started.

| | How To ... |
|---|---|
| Technology | upload photos from a camera to a computer |
| Crafts | build a cat-scratch pole |
| Cooking | make pancakes |
| Daily Living | give yourself a manicure |
| Health and Fitness | set up a weekly schedule of swim workouts |

2.  After five minutes, stop brainstorming and review the table. Circle the idea that you would like to write about. Be sure to select a process that can be clearly explained in 350 to 400 words.

**Gather Ideas and Details.** Think through the process that you want to write about. If possible, complete the process and take notes on what you do. On separate paper, list each main step.

Here is how one writer listed the steps in setting up a swimmer's workout.

--Choose a location to swim.

--Choose three days per week to swim.

--Choose a set time per day to swim.

--Set up a training session for working on your swimmer's form.

--Do that session two times per week.

--Set up a session for working on your endurance as a swimmer.

--Do that session once per week.

**T!p** After you gather ideas and details, think about the amount of material you have. Is there too little for your target word count? Just enough? Far too much? If necessary, narrow your topic or choose a different process to explain. The extra work will take more time, but it will help you meet the requirements of the assignment.

**Organize Ideas and Details.** Organize the steps in your article by making a sequence chain. A sequence chain lists each main step in the process, with substeps listed below the main steps.

1. Plan your workout schedule.
   a. Choose a location to swim.
   b. Choose three days per week to swim.
   c. Choose a set time per day to swim.

2. Set up a training session for working on your swimmer's form.
   a. Warm-up: 4 x 25 yards
   b. Workout: 10 x 25 yards
   c. Cooldown: 2 x 25 yards
   d. Do that session two times per week.

3. Set up a session for working on your endurance as a swimmer.
   a. Warm-up: 4 x 25 yards
   b. Workout: 2 x 25 yards with pull buoy, and 6 x 25 yards with rest points
   c. Cooldown: 2 x 25 yards
   d. Do that session once per week.

> **T!p**
>
> While writing the sequence chain, you may realize that the previous list you made left out some steps. It's okay now to add a main step or regroup steps.

## Draft

When writing a how-to article, use a friendly, helpful tone. A few strategies will help you create this tone.

- Use simple, everyday words instead of "big" words that may confuse your reader.
- If you must use a specialized word or term, don't forget to define it for your reader.
- Use the second-person point of view so you can speak directly to your reader.

When using these strategies, it is important to use each one consistently. For instance, don't use simple words in one paragraph and then use difficult technical terms in the next paragraph.

**Write Your How-To Article.** Write your how-to article, using the sequence chain you created as your outline.

- Write an introduction that introduces the topic of your article, and write a conclusion that brings the article to a close.
- Use a friendly, helpful tone throughout the article.
- Use transition words such as *first*, *next*, and *after that* to help your reader follow the sequence of steps. You can find a list of useful transition words in the table on pages 43–44.

Here is a paragraph from the article about setting up a beginner's swim workout. Notice how the writer makes changes to create a friendly tone and to add transitions.

Second, plan what to do in each of the three workouts. On the first swim day of the week, work on your swimmer's form. To start, Warm up by swimming two laps in a 25-yard-long pool, for a total of 100 yards. (All instructions in this article are based on a 25-yard pool.) Next, Swim five more laps. For each lap, practice a different stroke that you are learning. Cool down by swimming one lap (50 yards) slowly and easily.

If you are tired, use the kickboard for one lap. Finally,

## Revise

You can strengthen your article by correcting sentence fragments and run-ons. The following mini-lesson explains this strategy.

# Mini-Lesson: Correcting Sentence Fragments and Run-ons

During the revision stage of your writing process, find and correct sentences that have mistakes in structure. Two common mistakes are *sentence fragments* and *run-on sentences*.

➡ A **sentence fragment** is a group of words that begins with a capital letter and ends with end punctuation, but that is missing a subject, a verb, or both.

In the examples below, each subject is underlined once, and each verb is underlined twice.

Fragment: Stretches for a length of 25 yards. (no subject)
Correct: A pool lane stretches for a length of 25 yards.

Fragment: One lap, the same as two lengths of the pool. (no verb)
Correct: One lap equals two lengths of the pool.

Fragment: First, a location for your swim workouts. (no subject, no verb)
Correct: First, find a location for your swim workouts. (The subject, *you*, is understood.)

➡ A **run-on sentence** is formed of two or more sentences run together with no punctuation or conjunction to join them.

Run-on: Buy some good goggles and a kickboard these are helpful.
Correct: Buy some good goggles and a kickboard, **for** these are helpful.
Correct: Buy some good goggles and a kickboard; these are helpful.

Run-on: If you have long hair, use a swim cap it keeps your hair out of your eyes.
Correct: If you have long hair, use a swim cap. It keeps your hair out of your eyes.

## Give It a Try: Correct Sentence Fragments and Run-ons

On separate paper, rewrite the following paragraph. Correct each sentence fragment and run-on to form a complete, correct sentence. When you are finished, explain your revisions in a class discussion.

Just like with any sport. When you start out as a swimmer you need to start out slowly. This gives you time to work on your technique and build up your endurance, bit by bit. By starting slowly, you avoid getting burned out. And the chance to develop love for the sport. If you are ready to start a beginning swim program. Here is how you do it.

## Give It a Try: Correct Sentence Fragments and Run-ons in Your Article

Work with a partner to find and correct sentence fragments and run-ons in your how-to article. Follow these steps.

1. Exchange drafts with your writing partner.

2. Read your partner's draft and underline each fragment and run-on that you see.

3. Return the draft to its writer.

4. Look at the sentences that are underlined in your draft. Decide whether each one is a fragment or a run-on and revise it to make it complete and correct.

**Revise Your How-To Article.** Use the following checklist to revise the rough draft of your how-to article. The How-To Article Rubric that follows the checklist will help you determine how strong your article is and where to make revisions.

## Ideas

❑ Does the article explain how to accomplish one specific goal?

❑ Does each step clearly relate to this process? Check that each sentence is focused on the main goal.

## Organization

❑ Do you explain the steps in the order in which they should be completed? Rearrange any steps that are out of order.

## Voice

❑ Find three words or phrases that demonstrate a friendly, helpful tone. Write *voice* above them. Cross out any words that do not fit this tone.

❑ Do you use the second-person point of view consistently?

## Word choice

❑ Circle three transition words you used to show the sequence of steps. Add more if necessary.

❑ Circle three specific nouns and verbs you used to make your ideas clear. If necessary, revise nouns and verbs to make them more specific.

## Sentence fluency

❑ Have you used imperative sentences to tell the reader what to do? Find two and write *imper.* above them.

❑ Have you used declarative sentences to give information? Find two and write *decl.* above them.

# How-To Article Rubric

| | 4 Strong | 3 Effective | 2 Developing | 1 Beginning |
|---|---|---|---|---|
| **Ideas** | One process is explained. Each step clearly relates. | One process is explained. Most steps clearly relate. | One process is explained, but many steps do not relate. | The process is not clear. Most steps do not relate. |
| **organization** | Each step in the process is explained in sequential order. | Most steps are explained in sequential order. | Steps in the process are explained, but many are out of order. | Few steps in the process are explained, and their order is random. |
| **voice** | The writer uses a friendly tone and consistent point of view. | The friendly tone and point of view are mostly consistent. | A few sentences use a friendly tone; point of view is inconsistent. | The tone is not friendly, and point of view is inconsistent. |
| **word choice** | Transition words and specific nouns and verbs are used skillfully. | Many transition words and specific nouns and verbs are used. | A few transition words or specific nouns and verbs are used. | Transition words and specific nouns and verbs are absent. |
| **sentence fluency** | A useful mix of imperative and declarative sentences is used. | Some imperative and declarative sentences are used. | A few imperative sentences are used. | More imperative sentences are needed. |
| **conventions** | Few errors in capitalization, spelling, punctuation, or grammar are present. | Several errors in capitalization, spelling, punctuation, or grammar are present. | Errors in capitalization, spelling, punctuation, and grammar do not prevent understanding. | Errors in capitalization, spelling, punctuation, and grammar prevent understanding. |

## Edit

Edit the revised copy of your how-to article. The following questions will help you decide what to change, remove, or leave in place.

### Conventions
- ❑ Did you use a comma when you joined sentences with a co-ordinating conjunction?
- ❑ Did you use a comma when you began a sentence with a subordinate clause?
- ❑ Did you correct spelling mistakes, either with a friend's help or by using a dictionary?
- ❑ Did you correct grammar mistakes, either with a friend's help or by using a grammar handbook?

## PUBLISH

**Presentation.** Prepare your how-to article for publication by neatly writing or typing the final, edited copy.

**Publish Your Article.** Here are some ideas for publishing your how-to article.
- ❑ Draw diagrams or take photographs that illustrate your how-to process. Use your article and the images to create a brochure.
- ❑ Create a Web page where you and classmates can post your how-to articles.
- ❑ Create a demonstration video based on your how-to article. Ask a friend to film you as you perform the process that your article explains. As you work, have another friend provide the voice-over by reading your how-to article aloud.
- ❑ Have a how-to party with friends. At the party, pass out copies of your article and, if possible, show how to perform the steps in your article. Add to the fun by asking friends to bring and demonstrate their own how-to articles.

## Evaluate Your Article

Your teacher will either assess your article, ask you to self-assess your article, or ask you to switch with a partner and assess each other's work.

## Evaluate the Model Article.

Work with a partner to evaluate the following how-to article. Use the rubric on page 80 and write your score here: _____. In a class discussion, explain the score that you gave.

### How to Set up a Weekly Workout as a Beginning Swimmer

Just like with any sport, when you start out as a swimmer you need to start out slowly. This gives you time to work on your technique and build up your endurance, bit by bit. By starting slowly, you avoid getting burned out and you give yourself the chance to develop love for the sport. If you are ready to start a beginning swim program, here is how you do it.

First, plan which days of the week you will swim. Three days is a good number. Space the days apart so that you can rest in between. For instance, if you are using a pool at school, then Monday, Wednesday, and Friday afternoons might work. If you can go to a community pool, like at the YMCA, you could do Tuesday, Thursday, and Saturday. The point is, choose three days and specific times, and stick to the schedule.

Second, plan what to do in each of the three

workouts. On the first swim day of the week, work on your swimmer's form. To start, warm up by swimming two laps in a 25-yard-long pool, for a total of 100 yards. (All instructions in this article are based on a 25-yard pool.) Next, swim five more laps. For each lap, practice a different stroke that you are learning. If you are tired, use the kickboard for one lap. Finally, cool down by swimming one lap (50 yards) slowly and easily.

On your second workout day, perform the same routine as you did on day 1.

On your third workout day, focus on improving your endurance. Swim your warm-up set of two laps. Next, swim one lap using the pull buoy (a flotation device). Then swim three laps in this sequence: 25 yards, rest, 50 yards, rest, 50 yards, rest, 25 yards, rest. Finish by swimming a one-lap cooldown.

Follow this routine three days a week for at least a month before you increase the laps or difficulty. Don't burn out by pushing yourself too hard. Remember that beginning any training routine means learning the sport, but it means learning to love the sport too!

# Write an Explanatory Essay

When you write an **explanatory essay**, your purpose is to explain, or make clear, a topic for your reader. This type of writing often explains a specific perspective, opinion, or experience that the writer has. For example, here are some questions that an explanatory essay may answer:

*How do you feel about your school's dress code?*
*What do you enjoy about your favorite pastime?*
*What is the most generous action you have seen someone take?*

If you have ideas, opinions, and information about these questions, then you are already prepared to write an explanatory essay. In fact, you have probably written many explanations in your life already, both in and out of school. This chapter will help you strengthen your skills of explanatory writing.

## Six Traits of an Explanatory Essay

| Ideas | The topic is focused. Reasons and examples make the topic clear. |
|---|---|
| organization | Reasons and examples are arranged with care, such as in order of importance. |
| voice | The writer's voice shows confidence in the topic and an eagerness to help the reader understand. |
| word choice | Vivid, specific words make the writer's ideas memorable. |
| sentence fluency | A variety of sentence structures and lengths creates a pleasing rhythm to the writing. |
| conventions | Capitalization, spelling, punctuation, and grammar are correct. |

In the model paragraph below, the writer explains her opinion about technology.

> One of the biggest challenges facing teenagers today is the pressure to own technology. Why the pressure? For one reason, technology touches every part of our lives, including how we talk to our friends. When our parents were in school, they communicated by writing notes and letters. Nowadays, teenagers use e-mail, instant messages, and social-networking Web sites. In addition, technical gadgets like these are exciting and fun to own, but they are expensive, too. Some people cannot afford all these gadgets; some people don't want to spend their money on them. Despite its benefits, technology can be a burden to a tech-smart generation.

## Give It a Try: Examine the Model Paragraph

Working with a partner, use the model paragraph above to answer the following questions. Write your answers on separate paper.

1. **Ideas.** What main idea is the writer explaining?
2. **Organization.** What reasons does the writer give to explain the main idea? Copy two sentences from the paragraph that express two main reasons.
3. **Voice and word choice.** What conclusion can you draw about the writer's age, based on this paragraph? Explain.
4. **Sentence fluency.** Copy one sentence that begins with an introductory element and circle this element.
5. **Conventions.** List three rules of comma usage that the writer follows.

# Your Turn to Write: Compose an Explanatory Essay

Now you'll write an essay in which you explain something to an audience. Read the assignment carefully and follow the strategies and instructions for each stage of the writing process.

## Assignment

*Tech-Teen Online*, a Web site for young people under age 20, has announced its theme for next month's home page: technology and teens. The Web site's editor invites essays that describe the role of technology in the writer's life. Questions for thought include these: How do you use technology? Do you enjoy using technology? What do you love and hate about technology? Which form of technology do you wish you could remove from your life?

Write an essay of 350–400 words for *Tech-Teen Online* in which you explain the role of technology in your life.

## Prewrite

**Analyze the Prompt.** What does the prompt tell you about your goals for this assignment? Reread the assignment closely and answer the following questions. Write your answers on separate paper.

1. What is the purpose of this essay?
2. Who is the audience for this essay?
3. How long does the essay need to be?

**Gather Ideas and Details.** With your teacher's permission, gather in a small group. Take five minutes to discuss the role of technology in your lives. These sentence starters will help you begin.

- The first thing that comes to mind when I hear the word *technology* is . . .
- The thing I love about technology is . . .
- The thing I hate about technology is . . .
- I can't survive a day without . . .
- One form of technology that costs too much is . . .

During the discussion, jot down ideas about technology in young people's lives. In addition to your own ideas, it's okay to list ideas from others that you would like to use.

**Organize Ideas and Details.** Look over the ideas that you wrote down during the activity above. Circle 3 or 4 of the strongest ideas to use in your essay. Then number these ideas in order of priority, from least to most important. Think about the list you have formed. Ask yourself these questions:

- ❑ Do you have 3 or 4 solid ideas about technology in your life to explain in your essay?
- ❑ Do you have reasons or examples to support and explain each idea?
- ❑ Do you have too many ideas to explain in this essay? If so, which 3–4 ideas would your readers most want to read about?
- ❑ If you don't have enough ideas listed, what can you add to your list?
- ❑ Do you need to change the order of importance of the ideas so that the strongest, most important idea is listed last?

In the example on the next page, the writer has listed three ideas about the role of technology in her life. Beneath each main idea, she has listed supporting examples.

Technology in My Life

1. Technology helps me.
    --Internet research for school projects
    --Cell phone for emergencies

2. Technology hurts me.
    --I can't afford everything I want
    --It makes my friends seem like robots sometimes

3. I can't live without technology.
    --I need my music player.
    --I need to stay connected to friends.
       phone
       e-mail
       instant messages
       social networking page

 Draft

An effective explanatory essay hinges on a strong thesis statement. The following mini-lesson will help you write a strong thesis statement for your essay on technology in your life.

## Mini-Lesson: Writing a Thesis Statement

You have probably heard many times that the introduction in an essay should hook the reader's interest. This is true. However, the introduction must go one step farther. It must also state exactly what the essay will explain or show to be true. This statement is called the *thesis statement*.

   A **thesis statement** declares exactly what the body of the essay will explain or prove.

Here is an example of a thesis statement.

One of the biggest challenges facing teenagers today is the pressure to own technology.

The essay that follows this thesis statement should explain *why* the pressure to own technology is a challenge in teenagers' lives.

Here is another thesis statement.

Technology helps me and technology hurts me, and the truth is, I can't live without it.

The essay that follows this thesis statement should explain *how* technology helps the writer, *how* it hurts the writer, and *why* the writer cannot live without it.

As you can see in the above examples, a strong thesis statement is *focused*. The thesis statement makes a statement or claim that is narrow enough to be fully explained or proved in the essay.

Too Broad: *Everybody uses technology, whether they like it or not.* (The idea of everybody is too broad to prove in an essay.)

Focused: *Whether I like it or not, I cannot get through a day without using a computer, a cell phone, or a digital music player.* (This thesis statement narrows the topic to one person––the writer––and to three specific types of technology.)

A strong thesis statement is a complete sentence that does two things: It identifies a topic, and it states something specific about the topic.

Just a topic: *Technology.*

Just a topic: *This essay is about technology.*

A thesis statement: *Technology keeps me connected to friends, information, and music.* (This statement identifies the topic of technology and states three reasons why the writer uses technology.)

## Give It a Try: **Write a Thesis Statement**

Write your answer to each question on separate paper.

1. What is the topic of your explanatory essay?
2. What are the main ideas that you will explain in the essay?
3. Using the information in questions 1 and 2, write a thesis statement for your explanatory essay.

**Write Your Explanatory Essay.** Now that you have gathered ideas and details, planned the organization of your essay, and written a thesis statement, you are ready to write your explanatory essay. Here are a few tips to keep in mind as you write:

- The first paragraph of your essay should include a thesis statement.
- Each body paragraph should explain one main idea about the role of technology in your life. These paragraphs should be arranged in order from least to most important.
- The concluding paragraph should offer a final thought about technology in your life.

**T!p** Give your essay a title that gets your reader's attention and hints at the topic. An effective title may use a key word from the essay, ask a question that the essay answers, or use an interesting phrase or expression to make the reader want to read more.

 **Revise**

Use the following checklist to revise the rough draft of your explanatory essay. The Explanatory Essay Rubric that follows the checklist will help you determine how strong your essay is and where to make revisions.

## Ideas

- ❏ Place a check mark next to your thesis statement if it identifies a focused topic and says something important about it. If not, revise it.
- ❏ Underline two reasons and examples that support each main idea.

## Organization

- ❏ Make sure that you arranged ideas in order from least to most important.

## Voice

- ❏ Do you use a confident tone and show that you are eager to explain this topic? Write *voice* above words and phrases that demonstrate this tone.

## Word choice

- ❏ Circle three transition words or phrases that help show the order of importance.
- ❏ Circle three vivid, specific words you used. Revise any plain or weak words.

## Sentence fluency

- ❏ Check that you used a variety of sentence structures and sentence lengths.

# Explanatory Essay Rubric

| | 4 Strong | 3 Effective | 2 Developing | 1 Beginning |
|---|---|---|---|---|
| **Ideas** | One topic is explained using reasons or examples. | Most reasons and examples help to explain the topic. | Some reasons and examples help to explain the topic. | The topic and the reasons or examples are unclear. |
| **organization** | Ideas are arranged in order of importance. | One idea seems out of place. | Ideas are in no particular order. | The order of ideas is confusing. |
| **voice** | The writer uses a confident tone, drawing the reader in. | Most paragraphs have a confident tone. | A mixture of confident and uncertain tones is used. | The writer's tone is uncertain and hesitant. |
| **word choice** | Vivid, specific words make the writer's ideas memorable. | Some vivid, specific words are used. | One or two vivid, specific words are used. | Key words are general, plain, or misused. |
| **sentence fluency** | A variety of sentence structures and lengths are used. | There is some variety in sentence structure and length. | A few sentences begin with an introductory element. | Sentence structure is repetitive and mechanical. |
| **conventions** | Few errors in capitalization, spelling, punctuation, or grammar are present. | Several errors in capitalization, spelling, punctuation, or grammar are present. | Errors in capitalization, spelling, punctuation, and grammar do not prevent understanding. | Errors in capitalization, spelling, punctuation, and grammar prevent understanding. |

## Edit

Edit the revised copy of your essay. The following questions will help you decide what to change, remove, or leave in place.

### Conventions
❏ Did you use commas to separate words, phrases, or clauses in a series?
❏ Did you use a comma when you joined sentences with a co-ordinating conjunction?
❏ Did you use a comma when you began a sentence with an introductory element?
❏ Did you correct spelling mistakes, either with a friend's help or by using a dictionary?
❏ Did you correct grammar mistakes, either with a friend's help or by using a grammar handbook?

## PUBLISH

**Presentation.** Prepare your explanatory essay for publication by writing or typing the final, edited copy.

**Publish Your Essay.** Here are some ideas for publishing your explanatory essay.
❏ Submit the essay for publication in your school newspaper.
❏ With your teacher's permission, hang a copy of your essay on a bulletin board in your classroom.
❏ Use the essay as the first entry in a blog.

## Evaluate Your Essay

Your teacher will either assess your essay, ask you to self-assess your essay, or ask you to switch with a partner and assess each other's work.

# Evaluate the Model Essay

Work with a partner to evaluate the following explanatory essay. Use the rubric on page 93 and write your score here: _____. In a class discussion, explain the score that you gave.

### Love, Hate, and Technology

As a teenager from an average American family, I cannot escape technology. I see it at home and at school, the two places where I spend most of my time. And when I go to a store, to a movie, or to a friend's house, I see technology there, too. All around me are gadgets and wires and beeps and whirs. Technology helps me and technology annoys me, and the truth is, I can't live without it.

One of the most helpful things about technology is that it makes life easier. For example, when I need to research aardvarks, or find out who Patrick Henry was, I can use the Internet. The Internet is full of helpful, reliable sources of information. There are encyclopedias, dictionaries, biographies, and topic-oriented Web sites. Another example of how technology makes life easier is the use of cell phones for emergencies. I carry a cell phone with me at all times. I know that if I need my mom or dad, all I have to do is dial their number, and they'll pick up their cell phone.

Technology is helpful, but it is annoying, too. For one thing, technology is like a puppy that won't stop jumping on you. It's always in my face. This is annoying because I cannot afford all the technology that is advertised. These ads make me think I can't live without a better cell phone, a music player with more storage room, or a personal-sized DVD player. It's annoying to see all these great things but not be able to buy them. In addition, I have friends who can't tear themselves away from technology for an instant, and it makes them seem like robots. Instead of hanging out with me in person, they sit in front of some form of technology and send me instant messages. A robot could do that.

From my perspective, technology plays a helpful role in my life, and it plays an annoying role too. But overall, I can't live without technology. If I could choose to get rid of it all, I would not. I need my cell phone, my computer, my e-mail program, my instant messages, and the Web sites where I post photos and look at friends' photos. Technology helps me to be me, and I won't give that up.

# Chapter 7

# Write a Cause-and-Effect Essay

We notice causes and effects every day. For example, imagine that you get a new haircut. The next day at school, several people say, "You look great!" You might wonder what caused this positive response. Then you'd remember your haircut.

*cause:* haircut
*effect:* compliments about how you look

Or let's say that you put a DVD into the player and press Play. The film starts, then freezes. You wonder, "Why did that happen?" You remove the DVD and find scratches on it.

*cause:* scratches on the DVD
*effect:* the film freezes

In this chapter, you will have the opportunity to examine causes and effects in your daily life and to write about one specific cause-and-effect relationship.

## Six Traits of a Cause-and-Effect Essay

| Ideas | The writer identifies a specific cause-and-effect relationship. |
|---|---|
| Organization | The article includes a strong beginning, a middle that is organized logically, and a strong conclusion. |
| Voice | The writer's voice is interesting and knowledgeable. |
| Word Choice | Transitions help to make the cause-and-effect relationship clear. Vivid words help to make key ideas memorable. |
| Sentence Fluency | A variety of sentence types and structures creates a pleasing rhythm to the writing. |
| Conventions | Capitalization, spelling, punctuation, and grammar are correct. |

In the paragraph below, the author explains effects of stress on his performance on tests in school.

Time after time, I would study for a test, learn the material, and then perform poorly on the test because of stress. Stress affected me in three ways. First, stress caused me to lose sleep the night before a test. As a result, I was tired and unfocused on test day. Second, stress caused me to feel sick to my stomach. I couldn't eat, and then I felt hungry *and* sick on test day. Third, stress caused me to focus on my fear of failure instead of on my knowledge. As a result, my mind went blank whenever I read a hard question. Even though I knew the answer, I was too afraid of failing to relax enough to remember the answer. The effects of stress became such a big problem that I decided to learn how to overcome stress.

## Give It a Try: Examine the Model Paragraph

Use the model paragraph above to answer the following questions. Write your answers on separate paper. Then, in a class discussion, explain your answers.

1. **Ideas.** What cause-and-effect relationship does the writer explain?
2. **Organization.** List three effects of stress that the writer lists.
3. **Voice and word choice.** List three words that you think are especially vivid or strong.
4. **Sentence fluency.** Explain one strategy the writer uses to create sentence variety.
5. **Conventions.** The writer uses forms of the words *affect* (verb) and *effect* (noun). *Affect* can also be a noun, and *effect* can also be a verb. Consult a dictionary and write the four definitions, along with their pronunciations.

## Your Turn to Write: Compose a Cause-and-Effect Essay

Now you'll write your own essay in which you explain a cause and its effects. Read the assignment carefully and follow the strategies and instructions for each stage of the writing process.

## Assignment

Some of the personal decisions we make affect other people as well as ourselves. For example, you might decide to join the basketball team. As a result, you get to play a sport you love, but your best friend feels abandoned. Or perhaps you decide to dance for fitness in your room each afternoon. As a result, you feel great, but your downstairs neighbor becomes angry at the loud music and the banging on her ceiling.

Write an essay of 350–400 words in which you explain a choice that you made and how it affected yourself as well as others. Your teacher may ask you to read your essay aloud to your classmates.

## Prewrite

**Analyze the Prompt.** What does the prompt tell you about your goals for this assignment? Reread the assignment closely and answer the following questions. Write your answers on separate paper.

1. What is the purpose of this essay?
2. Who is the audience for this essay?
3. How long does the essay need to be?

**Choose a Topic.** In the table on the next page, list three decisions you have made. Next to each decision, list effects of the decision. Finally, choose one of the cause-and-effect relationships to be the topic of your essay. Draw a star beside your choice.

## Cause-and-Effects Chart

| CAUSE<br>A decision I made: | | EFFECTS<br>Results of the decision: |
|---|---|---|
| | → | |
| | → | |
| | → | |

**Gather Ideas and Details.** Explore your cause-and-effect relationship in more detail by writing responses in the table below.

## Cause-and-Effect Relationship

| |
|---|
| A brief description of the cause (my decision): |
| Details of Effect 1: |
| Details of Effect 2: |
| Details of Effect 3: |
| My response or reaction to my decision and its effects: |

**Organize Ideas and Details.** Using information in the cause-and-effect relationship table, plan the organization of your essay. Useful strategies include a beginning-middle-end table and an outline (formal or informal). Choose one of these methods and complete your work on a separate sheet of paper.

## Draft

When you write the draft of your cause-and-effect essay, keep these tips in mind.

- **Start strong.** Begin your essay with a paragraph that makes your reader care about your topic and that includes a thesis statement.

- **Move from least to most important effect.** In the body paragraphs, explain the least significant effect first. Build on that by explaining a more significant effect. Keep the reader interested by building on that with an even more important effect.

- **Finish strong.** Conclude your essay with a paragraph that expresses your response to the cause-and-effect relationship you have just described. Are you proud of your decision? Do you regret it? Did the effects of your decision cause you to make yet another decision? Express this final response briefly.

**Write Your Cause-and-Effect Essay.** Use your prewriting ideas and your outline to write a well-organized cause-and-effect essay.

## Revise

You have planned and written the first draft of a cause-and-effect essay. Those stages of the writing process require a great deal of time, thought, and work. You should feel a well-deserved sense of accomplishment—but don't stop your work yet! Now, during the revision stage, you can make your draft stronger and more forceful. One way to do this is to replace weak or overused words with more vivid, precise choices. The following mini-lesson explains this revision strategy.

## Mini-Lesson: Revising Weak and Overused Words

Once you have written the first draft of an essay, you can breathe a sigh of satisfaction that you captured your ideas in writing. After that, take a second look at how you expressed these ideas. Which words are so often used that they are weak, tired, or virtually invisible? These words can pull your ideas down to their level, making your ideas seem weak or tired, too.

To make your writing—and therefore your ideas—more forceful, replace weak words with forceful ones.

Review the lists of weak and overly used words in the table below. As you read each word, ask yourself, "What is a more vivid word that could take the place of this word?" The contrast between the weak words and the strong ones you discover may surprise and inspire you.

| Instead of this word . . . | . . . use this word | Instead of this word . . . | . . . use this word |
|---|---|---|---|
| a lot | | nice | |
| bad | | old | |
| big | | pretty | |
| fine | | quite | |
| fun | | really | |
| good | | sad | |
| great | | so | |
| happy | | very | |
| interesting | | walk | |
| just | | well | |

# Give It a Try: Replace Weak and Overused Words

Use a thesaurus and your own knowledge to find vivid words to replace *five* words in the table on the previous page. Write your replacements in the table. Then, in a class discussion, learn about vivid, expressive words that other people have discovered. Write these ideas in the table, too.

# Give It a Try: Replace Weak and Overused Words in Your Essay

Work with a partner to identify weak or overused words in your essay. Underline each one. You may find one or two examples, or you may find a long list of examples. On your own, replace each underlined word with a more vivid or forceful word.

**Revise Your Cause-and-Effect Essay.** Use the following checklist to revise the rough draft of your essay. The Cause-and-Effect Essay Rubric that follows the checklist will help you determine how strong your essay is and where to make revisions.

### Ideas
❑ Does the essay focus on one specific cause-and-effect relationship? Underline the sentence where you introduce the relationship.
❑ Place a check mark above each detail that helps to explain the cause or effect, or helps to make the cause-effect relationship clear. Revise or cross out any irrelevant details.

### Organization
❑ Check that you have a strong beginning, a middle that is organized logically, and a strong conclusion. Revise or add parts as necessary.

### Voice

❑ As a writer, do you sound interesting and knowledgeable to your reader? Write *voice* above three words or phrases that demonstrate this.

### Word choice

❑ Circle three transition words to show how causes and effects link to one another.

❑ Circle three vivid, forceful words. Revise any weak words.

### Sentence fluency

❑ Check that each of your sentences is complete.

❑ Check that you used a variety of sentence types, sentence structures, and sentence lengths.

# Cause-and-Effect Essay Rubric

| | 4 Strong | 3 Effective | 2 Developing | 1 Beginning |
|---|---|---|---|---|
| **Ideas** | The essay explains a specific cause-and-effect relationship using relevant details. | The essay explains a cause-and-effect relationship. Most details are relevant. | The writer describes a cause or some effects, but the relationship is unclear. | The writer explains ideas that do not connect in a cause-and-effect manner. |
| **Organization** | Details are arranged from least to most important. | A few details are out of place. | It is clear which idea is most important, but other ideas are in no particular order. | Details are offered in no particular order. |
| **Voice** | The tone is interesting and knowledgeable. | In most paragraphs the tone is interesting and knowledgeable. | Some sentences show the writer's attempt to be interesting or knowledgeable. | The tone is stiff, bored, preachy, or otherwise uninteresting. |
| **Word Choice** | Transitions and vivid words are used skillfully. | Some transitions and vivid words are present. | Two or three transitions or vivid words are present. | Transitions are absent. More vivid, forceful words are needed. |
| **Sentence Fluency** | Sentences are complete. A variety of sentence types is used. | One or two sentences are incomplete. A variety of sentence types is used. | Many sentences are incomplete. There is some variety of sentence types. | Sentences are mostly of one type or are incomplete. |
| **Conventions** | Capitalization, spelling, punctuation, and grammar are correct. | Several errors in capitalization, spelling, punctuation, or grammar are present. | Errors in capitalization, spelling, punctuation, and grammar do not prevent understanding. | Errors in capitalization, spelling, punctuation, and grammar prevent understanding. |

**Edit**

To edit your writing means to find and correct mistakes in capitalization, spelling, punctuation, and grammar. Here are three strategies for identifying mistakes in your writing:

**Use a checklist.** Use the checklists in the editing sections in this book. Use checklists that your teacher provides. Use checklists that you create based on your own particular needs.

**Listen to your essay.** Make two copies of your essay and pair up with a partner. As your partner reads your essay aloud, follow along on your copy. Listen for incomplete sentences. Listen for times when your reader stumbles over a word that is spelled incorrectly or stumbles over a sentence that needs one or more commas. Circle each mistake so that you can go back later and fix it.

**Highlight punctuation marks.** Highlight each punctuation mark in your essay. Then consider each mark, one by one. Ask, "Did I use this mark correctly?" and "Is this the best mark to use here?" If you're not sure about the use of a mark, look it up in a handbook.

**Read.** Develop an ear for correct grammar, such as subject-verb agreement and correct pronoun references, by reading for pleasure. The more you read strong writing, the more familiar the traits of writing will become—and the easier it will be to spot and correct mistakes in conventions in your own writing.

**Edit Your Cause-and-Effect Essay.** Edit the revised copy of your cause-and-effect essay. The following questions will help you decide what to change, remove, or leave in place.

**Conventions**
- ❏ Did you capitalize proper nouns?
- ❏ Did you use commas to separate words, phrases, or clauses in a series?
- ❏ Did you use a comma when you joined sentences with a coordinating conjunction?

❑ Did you use a comma when you began a sentence with an introductory element?

❑ Did you find and correct punctuation errors, either with a friend's help or by using a handbook?

❑ Did you correct spelling mistakes, either with a friend's help or by using a dictionary?

❑ Did you correct grammar mistakes, either with a friend's help or by using a grammar handbook?

## PUBLISH

**Presentation.** Prepare your essay for publication by writing or typing the final, edited copy.

**Publish Your Essay.** Here are ideas for publishing your cause-and-effect essay.

❑ Read your essay to your family. Ask them to tell you what they remember about the decision you explain in the essay.

❑ Post your essay as an entry in your blog.

❑ Submit your essay to an online magazine that publishes materials written by young people.

## Evaluate Your Essay

Your teacher will either assess your essay, ask you to self-assess your essay, or ask you to switch with a partner and assess each other's work.

## Evaluate the Model Essay

Work with a partner to evaluate the following cause-and-effect essay. Use the rubric on page 105 and write your score here: _____. In a class discussion, explain the score that you gave.

## The Price of Guitar Lessons

When I convinced my parents to pay for guitar lessons, I had no idea that the whole family would pay.

When I saw the ad for the lessons, I was ignited with joy. This was my chance to learn to play my favorite instrument! My parents said they did not have the money to pay for lessons, but I begged, cried, and persisted until they agreed. I started the lessons with a buzz of anticipation. I had a lesson every Friday after school.

That first Friday, I came home from my lesson looking forward to our traditional special Friday night dinner. I was a little surprised that we had macaroni and cheese, salad, and fruit. Then the next Friday we had spaghetti with marinara sauce, salad, and fruit. Again, nothing special. When the third Friday rolled around, I saw sandwiches and fruit on the dinner table. I had to ask. "Mom, why aren't we doing Pizza Friday or Steak Friday or Pot Roast Friday anymore?"

"By not paying for expensive Friday dinners, we can pay for your guitar lessons," she said. "Don't worry, it's worth it." I looked at my brother and sister.

I was shocked. Once I had time to think things over, I decided that I would pay for my own guitar lessons. I went to work doing yard work on Saturdays, and the family began having special Friday dinners once again.

# Test Writing: The Expository Essay

During your time in school, you will probably write many expository essays on tests. For instance, an English teacher may ask you to explain whether you agree or disagree with a character's actions in a novel. A history teacher may ask you to explain the causes of the American Revolution. Take a moment right now to list the topics of two expository responses that you have written for tests. Then share them with the class.

Whether it's a short response or a long one, expository writing allows you to show your writing skills while explaining your ideas or knowledge. The following table gives more information about the traits of writing and expository test writing.

## Six Traits of an Expository Test Essay

| | |
|---|---|
| Ideas | The topic is narrowed to a specific subject to be explained. Each detail clearly relates to the topic. |
| organization | Details are arranged with care, such as in order of importance, from general to specific, or order of steps in a sequence. |
| voice | The writing style fits with the purpose and audience of the explanation. |
| word choice | Specific nouns and verbs help the reader understand what the writer is explaining or how a process is completed. |
| sentence fluency | Declarative sentences are used to give information. A variety of sentence types and structures creates a pleasing rhythm to the writing. |
| conventions | Capitalization, spelling, punctuation, and grammar are correct. |

# Preparing to Write Your Test Essay

The first step in writing your test essay is to read the writing prompt carefully. The writing prompt usually gives you several types of information. This may include test-taking instructions, what type of essay to write (descriptive, explanatory, etc.), and what topic to write about. Here is an example of a prompt for an expository essay.

---

**Instructions**
You have 25 minutes to complete the written composition. Read the prompt below. Then use separate paper to plan and draft your composition. Only your draft will be scored.

**Writing Prompt**
In school, in sports, and in other activities, we work in teams to accomplish our goals. From your perspective, what makes a good team player? Write an essay in which you explain what makes a good team player in school, in a sport, or in another activity.

---

## 1. Study the Prompt
Before you begin to write your essay, take a few moments to study the prompt. You can sort through the information in the prompt by answering these questions:

**What is the purpose of the essay?** Scan the prompt for key words that tell you what kind of essay to write.

**Words That Signal an Expository Essay**
explain
tell
opinion
perspective
reasons
examples

**What should you write about?** Study the prompt to determine exactly what you must write. This information is usually stated in one key sentence, and it is often the last sentence of the prompt. In the prompt on page 110, the key sentence is this one:

*Write an essay in which you explain what makes a good team player in school, in a sport, or in another activity.*

The other sentences in the prompt help you understand your purpose for writing, but this sentence tells you exactly what you should write.

**How much time do you have to write?** According to the instructions, the student has 25 minutes to write the essay. If a prompt does not state a time limit, this information may be printed on another page in the test booklet, or your teacher may inform you of the time limit.

**What other instructions are stated?** Check the prompt for additional instructions. The prompt may include a reminder list of things to be sure to include in your essay.

## 2. Plan Your Time
After studying the prompt, make a quick plan for how to use your time. If you have 25 minutes to write the essay, you could use your time as follows:

5–7 minutes:    Study the prompt and complete the prewriting.

13–15 minutes: Write the essay.

5 minutes:       Revise and edit the essay.

### 3. Prewrite

During the time set aside for prewriting, you should gather ideas and details for your topic and organize the information.

**Gather ideas and details.** Use a few of your prewriting minutes to gather ideas and details. You may choose to use one of the following prewriting strategies.

TOOLKIT

In addition to freewriting and listing, useful prewriting strategies include
- idea map
- descriptive details table
- cause-and-effect chart

- **Freewriting.** Write your topic at the top of a sheet of paper. For three minutes, write about your topic without stopping. Let one idea lead to the next, and don't worry about spelling, grammar, or organization. After three minutes, stop writing and read your freewriting. Circle ideas and details that you could use in your essay.

- **Listing.** Write your topic at the top of a sheet of paper. Make several columns on your paper, such as *actions*, *attitudes*, and *skills*. Take three minutes to list as many details in each column as you can. Finally, review your lists and circle details that you could use in your essay.

The model below shows how one writer selected a topic (teamwork in volleyball) and listed ideas and details about the topic.

Teamwork in ~~group writing project,~~ volleyball, ~~planning a party for our parents~~

| Attitudes | Actions | Skills |
|---|---|---|
| positive | come to practice | quick-thinking |
| encouraging | work hard | quick-moving |
| supportive | listen to Coach | strong arms |
| gracious loser | play your position | limber muscles |
| gracious winner | don't hog the court | know all the rules |

T!p　During your prewriting work, it's easy to lose track of your goal and write down information that is off topic. You don't have time to waste by going off topic! To keep yourself on track, reread the writing prompt halfway through your prewriting session.

**Organize the information.** Use your remaining prewriting time to organize your information. During a 25-minute testing period, it is reasonable to plan for a 3- to 5-paragraph essay. To save time, use a simple graphic organizer such as the one below to group key points. Use your own ways of abbreviating words to save time.

---

*beginning*
--para. 1: Teamwork is using your attitudes and your
            actions to help your team do its best.

---

*middle*
(see prewriting for details)
--para. 2: Attitudes
--para. 3: Actions
--para. 4: Skills

---

*end*
--para. 5:
--sum up teamwork qualities
--Without teamwork, the team would be no fun and would
    probably lose all the time.

---

## Writing Your Test Essay

After studying the prompt, gathering ideas and details, and organizing your information, you are ready to write your essay. Rest assured that the time you spent doing prewriting will help you write more quickly and purposefully.

To keep yourself on track, follow the organizational plan you made during prewriting. Refer to it between paragraphs so that you don't go off track.

## Polishing Your Test Essay

During the last few minutes of your test period, review your essay to correct errors in capitalization, spelling, punctuation, and grammar. Mark your corrections directly on the copy to be scored, and make all marks neatly and cleanly. You don't want to lose points because someone couldn't make out your words due to a sloppy correction!

In the following model, the writer makes corrections to her introductory paragraph. She replaces weak words with stronger ones, corrects a sentence fragment, and corrects a misspelled word.

> Sometimes, the ~~best~~ most effective way to get what you want is to work with other people to get it. This is called Teamwork. In volleball, the only way to have fun and win games is for all team members to have practice the qualities of teamwork in their attitudes, their actions, and their skills.

## Evaluating an Expository Test Essay

When teachers evaluate your test essay, they know that you planned and wrote the essay in a short amount of time. Consequently, they do not expect a perfect essay. At the same time, they do expect you to show your knowledge of the traits of writing. They will look to see

- how completely you respond to the prompt
- how well you support your ideas with reasons and examples
- how clearly you organize your essay
- how you use voice to make your writing interesting

- how correctly you write sentences
- how correctly you use the conventions of writing

The following rubric shows guidelines for evaluating an expository test essay.

# Expository Test Essay Rubric

|  | 4<br>Strong | 3<br>Effective | 2<br>Developing | 1<br>Beginning |
|---|---|---|---|---|
| Ideas | The writer wrote to the prompt; reasons and examples are relevant. | The writer wrote to the prompt; most reasons and examples are relevant. | The writer included some relevant reasons and examples. | The writer did not write to the prompt. There are few reasons or examples. |
| organization | Information is arranged logically. | Most information is arranged logically. | Organization of information is awkward. | Information is included in no particular order. |
| voice | The writing style helps the reader connect to the explanation. | The writing style of some paragraphs draws the reader in. | The writing style of one or two sentences draws the reader in. | Writing is mechanical, making it hard for readers to connect. |
| word choice | Transitions and vivid words are used. | A few transitions and vivid words are used. | One or two transitions or vivid words are used. | No transitions or vivid words are used. |
| sentence fluency | Most sentences are complete. | A few sentences are incomplete. | Many sentences are incomplete. | Most sentences are incomplete. |
| conventions | Few errors in capitalization, spelling, punctuation, or grammar are present. | Several errors in capitalization, spelling, punctuation, or grammar are present. | Errors in capitalization, spelling, punctuation, and grammar do not prevent understanding. | Errors in capitalization, spelling, punctuation, and grammar prevent understanding. |

# Evaluate a Model Test Essay

Work with a partner to evaluate the following model essay. Use the rubric on page 115 and write your score here: _____. In a class discussion, explain the score that you gave.

## Teamwork in Volleball

Sometimes, the ~~best~~ [most effective] way to get what you want is to work with other people to get it. [This is called] Teamwork. In volleball, the only way to have fun and win games is for all team members to ~~have~~ [practice] the qualities of teamwork in their attitudes, their actions, and their skills.

A volleyball player's attitudes set the stage for the team's success. A player must show up to practice and to every game with a positive attitude. She must be encouraging and supportive to the other players, Even when they make mistakes or lose a point. If the team loses, each player should be a good sport and not blame each other. ~~Why?~~ ~~Because~~ blaming each other drags the team down. Also, when the team wins, it is good teamwork to be gracious winners. This means telling other players what they did well and congratulating the other team on being good opponents.

A volleball player's actions help the team be a success, too. This means coming to practice on time. [and] ~~Also~~ working hard. Sometimes a player just wants to show up and talk to her friends, but every minute of practice is a chance to ~~get better at the game~~ [improve] and help the team be stronger. At practice and in games, a player should listen to Coach, [because] the coach knows what is best for the team. Two important actions that show teamwork during a game is to play ~~you're~~ [your] position and don't hog the court. Knocking into each other and stealing the ball from each other usually loses points, and its not good teamwork.

Finally and most important a volleyball player's skills help build teamwork, too. Good skills help the team succeed, and that is what teamwork in a sport is all about. ~~That and having fun.~~ A skillful player must be quick‑thinking to respond to strong serves and sudden spikes of the ball. She must be quick‑moving to set or spike the ball before it drops to the floor. She must have strong arms for powerful moves and limber muscles to move easily. Above all, she should know the rules of the game, to serve her team well.

With these three things—attitudes, actions, and skills—a volleball player can be a ~~good~~ valuable team player. Without teamwork, the team would be no fun and would probably lose all the time.

## Write an Expository Test Essay

Now practice what you have learned by writing an expository essay in a testlike situation. Complete the following assignment.

**Instructions**
You have 25 minutes to complete the written composition. Read the prompt below. Then use separate paper to plan and draft your composition. Only your draft will be scored.

**Writing Prompt**
When people talk about courage, they often talk about actions taken during a war, a crisis, or an emergency. But how do people show courage in everyday life? Write an essay in which you explain what courage means to you and how someone has shown (or could show) courage in everyday life.

# Expository Writing Wrap-Up

The activities and information in these pages will help you continue to strengthen your expository-writing skills. In You Be the Judge, use the Expository Writing Rubric to evaluate a student's work. Ideas for Writing are additional expository-writing prompts you can use for practice. And finally, in the Unit 2 Reflections, you can list important ideas you have learned in this unit and set goals for future learning.

## You Be the Judge

Use what you've learned about the traits of expository writing to evaluate a student essay. First, review the traits of expository writing on page 67. Next, read the student essay printed below. Finally, in the rubric that follows the essay, assign the essay a score for each writing trait. In the space provided, explain each score that you assign.

### The Guide to a Dream Date

by yaychloe92, Bristow, VA

Excitement brews within every high school when the month of October approaches, and a frenzy of nervous anticipation occupies the minds of students as they debate on asking their dream date to the Homecoming Dance. How to avoid an awkward encounter with your crush as you pop the question? Well, there are a few helpful tips that should make asking that special someone a little less nerve-wracking. Even though your stomach is twisting in knots when you think about the disappointment you may face, portraying a cool, confident appearance is always key when talking to your potential date. Your crush is worth more effort than a simple asking as you pass each other in the hallway, so thinking of a creative and unique approach is also vital. Most importantly, avoid the embarrassment of rejection by asking a person that you know is actually interested in accompanying you to the dance. Every high-schooler dreads hearing a "no" or even worse, an "absolutely NOT!" answer from the person they work up the courage to extend themselves out to. By following these guidelines, it will help ensure a smooth Homecoming experience, avoid the agony of social death, and earn that "YES!"

When considering the ways to ask a potential Homecoming date, nervous butterflies may fill your stomach and produce nervous jitters that cause your brain to short-circuit, but this is completely normal for the unprepared teenager. One way to avoid this and keep your collected appearance when it actually comes time for "the asking," is to spend [time] each night before bed practicing your lines and facial expressions in a full length mirror. It is important to be in control of your body language, making sure not to sway uncomfortably from side to side, or startle your potential date with any sudden twitches. As you look at yourself in the mirror, practice a confident stance, placing both feet firmly on the ground, straightening your shoulders into good posture, and remembering to keep eye contact with the person you are speaking to. Rehearsing the lines you are going to say is also a useful tactic in avoiding an embarrassing encounter with your dream date. When preparing, try to eliminate any unusual noises, cracks in the voice, or loud snorts during a fake laugh that you use to fill an awkward silence. This will definitely increase the chances of wooing your crush into accepting your offer.

Standing out among the vast sea of students flooding the halls of your high school is no easy task, but uniqueness is imperative when asking a Homecoming date. If you like the person enough to want to spend an entire night of dancing with them, then they must be worth a little more creative effort than a conventional asking during an everyday, mundane encounter. Coming up with fun and innovative ideas will make you an even more desirable Homecoming commodity. Some examples of successful asking techniques include: 1) Writing your crush a trail of love notes, delivered to them in each class with a carnation, spelling out your desire to escort them to the dance, and meeting them at the end of the day to receive their answer. 2) Getting out of class early to decorate their car with balloons and streamers and writing "Homecoming?" on their window, then standing with a bouquet of roses until they come out of the building for you to surprise them in person. 3) Pulling some strings with the school administration and asking the question over the intercom during morning announcements. Being ambitious with the asking technique shows how much you desire to win over your date, and that you are enthusiastic about taking them to homecoming. Keep the method sweet and appropriate, remembering not to make it into an outrageously embarrassing experience for your crush.

Nothing is more uncomfortable than spending Homecoming with another person that you have nothing in common with. Having a plethora of background information is vital in selecting your Homecoming target. Instead of randomly asking a fellow classmate to accompany you at the last minute, take time to get to know another student that you are interested in, and pay attention to how they react to you as well. Strike up a conversation after class, or while "happening" to stand next to them in the lunch line, but avoid the corny pick-up lines like "Hey, what's cookin', good lookin'," which would most likely be returned with a dirty look of disgust in your direction. Instead, casually inquire information on their relationship status, but try to avoid seeming desperate. Asking a person that is already taken, or does not intend on going to the dance, is obviously useless. Observe how the conversation flows between you, and don't be afraid to flirt a little to let them know you are interested. If this person expresses your similar interests, and you get along well, then this might just be the perfect date! If there are too many awkward silences, and your encounters turned out unpleasantly, then this may unfortunately be a glimpse of what Homecoming would resemble.

Acquiring a date to Homecoming can be a traumatizing event if not handled in the proper way, but this advice will help to remedy any uneasiness you have about the asking process. By calming your nervous butterflies through preparation, taking a confident, ambitious approach to popping the question, and making sure your crush is really the right choice for you, these tips will almost guarantee an enjoyable night of dancing for you and your dream date. Rise above the chaos engulfing your school in the month of October, and make this a smooth Homecoming experience.

# Expository Writing Rubric

|  | 4 Strong | 3 Effective | 2 Developing | 1 Beginning |
|---|---|---|---|---|
| **Ideas** Score_____ | *explanation:* | | | |
| **organization** Score_____ | *explanation:* | | | |
| **voice** Score_____ | *explanation:* | | | |
| **word choice** Score_____ | *explanation:* | | | |
| **sentence fluency** Score_____ | *explanation:* | | | |
| **conventions** Score_____ | *explanation:* | | | |

# Ideas for Writing

The assignments that follow will give you additional practice with expository writing. Your teacher may choose one or let you pick one that's most interesting to you.

1. Most students are interested in ways to improve their performance in school. What are your secrets for getting your homework done on time, studying for a test, or learning difficult material? Write an essay of 350–400 words in which you explain

how to improve performance in school. Be sure to use examples to support your ideas.

2. As a young person, you may sometimes feel as if your life is out of your control. Older people make your rules and guide your life, and sometimes those people make mistakes. Write an essay of approximately 400 words in which you explain mistakes that adults make and how they can avoid them. Pay special attention to your voice in this essay, whether it is humorous, helpful, serious, or something else.

3. Natural disasters include earthquakes, floods, hurricanes, landslides, tsunamis, and volcanic eruptions. Choose one type of natural disaster and write a 400-word essay in which you explain this disaster to younger students. In your essay

   - give a basic definition of this type of disaster
   - explain at least one cause of the disaster
   - explain at least two effects of the disaster

4. When you read for pleasure, which genre (type) of writing do you turn to? Do you prefer mysteries, science fiction, graphic novels, or romances? Or perhaps you prefer poetry or plays. What is it about this type of writing that you enjoy? Write an essay of approximately 400 words in which you identify your favorite genre of writing and explain why you enjoy it. Your essay should be appropriate for presentation in your English class.

# Unit 2 Reflections

How are you different as a writer now that you have completed this unit on expository writing? What new knowledge do you have? How is your writing stronger? What kinds of things could you work on to become even stronger as an expository writer? Use the following space to reflect on your work in this unit and to set goals for the future.

## Focus on Me: My Achievements as an Expository Writer

What I've learned about expository writing in this unit:

Ways my expository writing is stronger now:

Things I can do to practice my skills of expository writing:

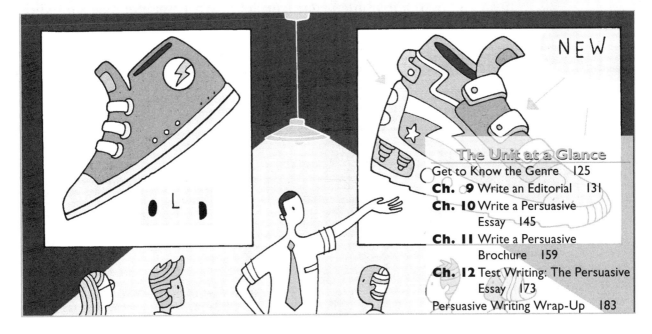

# Persuasive Writing

## Get to Know the Genre: Persuasive Writing

Topics as complex as war and as simple as the view through a window can spark different opinions in people. Think back over the conversations that you have had this week. Were there conversations in which you tried to convince a friend to take a certain action? Or conversations in which you tried to convince a parent to accept one of your opinions? What did you do or say to make a convincing case for your point of view?

Persuasive writing is much like spoken persuasion. In **persuasive writing**, the writer presents a case for or against an opinion, a viewpoint, or an action. A thesis statement, supporting reasons, and a memorable conclusion are essential ingredients.

# Give It a Try: Think About Prior Experience

Think of a time when you defended an opinion or viewpoint to someone who disagreed with you. What was the issue in question? In the following graphic organizer, jot down your memories of who said what.

| | |
|---|---|
| *The opinion or viewpoint that I defended was* | |
| *I said* | *and the other person said* |
| *I said* | *and the other person said* |
| *I said* | *and the other person said* |
| *I brought the discussion to a close by saying* | |

In this book, you have been learning about different forms of writing and the traits of writing. The table below explains more about the traits of persuasive writing.

# Six Traits of **Persuasive Writing**

| Ideas | The topic is narrowed to a specific position to be defended. Reasons and examples support the position. |
|---|---|
| Organization | The introduction states the writer's position. Body paragraphs give supporting reasons and respond to objections. The conclusion restates the position. |
| Voice | The writer's voice shows his or her concern or enthusiasm, balanced with a sense of trustworthiness. |
| Word Choice | Words are accurate. Descriptive words are fair. |
| Sentence Fluency | Sentences are complete. A variety of structures creates a pleasing rhythm. |
| Conventions | Capitalization, spelling, punctuation, and grammar are correct. |

## Real-World Example

Persuasive writing tries to convince readers to agree with an opinion or to take a particular action. The following paragraphs are taken from the article "Homework Does Not = A's" by Sara Bennett. In these paragraphs, Bennett tries to convince readers that homework may not be as helpful as some people think.

Be still when you have nothing to say; when genuine passion moves you, say what you've got to say, and say it hot.
—D. H. Lawrence
(British author, 1885–1930)

**Ideas:** the topic

**Word choice:** vivid verb

**Ideas:** the writer's opinion on the topic

**Organization:** The writer identifies the topic, then states her opinion, then gives supporting reasons.

Many parents are exasperated by how homework dominates their children's lives, even over the summer. But what they don't realize is that most studies find little correlation between homework and achievement in elementary school and only a moderate correlation in middle school. Even in high school, studies find that too much homework is counterproductive. . . .

Children need to play (one of the most important tasks of childhood according to child development experts), to eat dinner with their families (one of the biggest predictors of academic success), to talk with family and friends, to develop their passions and to read. These activities, not homework, will ensure that our children are happy and competitive in a highly competitive world.

**Conventions:** Parentheses enclose interrupting phrases.

**Sentence fluency:** interrupting phrase

**Ideas:** concluding thought

## Give It a Try: Examine the Real-World Example

Can you find additional examples of the traits of good writing in the model above? On separate paper, list three traits of writing. For each one, quote or describe an example from the model.

## Get Ready to Write

Now that you've explored the qualities of persuasive writing, you're ready to create some persuasive pieces of your own. In the chapters that follow, you'll write an editorial about a hot topic at your school, a persuasive essay about a green elective you'd like to see offered, a persuasive brochure describing a talent you can share, and a persuasive test essay about something you desire. You'll use the stages of the writing process—prewriting, drafting, revising, editing, and publishing—and you'll be presented with models and mini-lessons along the way.

As you work through these chapters, you can enrich your understanding by trying the suggestions below. These tips will help you connect what you're learning in this unit to your own life and the world around you.

### LEARNING TIPS

Read the editorials or opinion columns in newspapers. What topics do the writers cover? What tones do they use? How do they organize their articles?

Read brochures that you find in public buildings, offices, or other locations. Notice how brochures use few words, along with images, to persuade or inform readers.

Practice your persuasive skills in daily life. Persuade a parent to give you a special privilege. Persuade a brother or sister to trade chores with you. Send persuasive text messages or e-mails to friends and watch to see how effective you were.

Make a habit of sharing your opinions in conversations. Practice giving reasons why your opinion should be taken seriously. Pay attention to how your listeners respond.

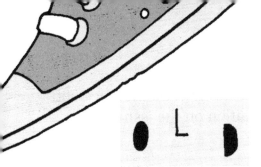

# Write an Editorial

Writing an editorial is an effective way to make sure that your opinion is heard. An **editorial** expresses the writer's opinions on a specific issue, usually a "hot topic" issue or issue that causes disagreement among people. Besides writing to express your opinions, you can write to inform people of facts on the issue and to help people figure out what *their* opinions are.

Most editorials are published in newspapers and magazines, either in print or online. Other editorials are published online as blog entries. In this chapter, you'll practice writing an editorial that is suitable for publication in a school newspaper.

## Six Traits of an **Editorial**

| Ideas | The topic is narrowed to the writer's position on an issue in the school or community. Reasons and examples are convincing. |
|---|---|
| organization | The introduction states the writer's position. Body paragraphs give convincing reasons and respond to objections. The conclusion restates the position. |
| voice | The writer demonstrates concern or enthusiasm, balanced with a sense of trustworthiness. |
| word choice | Words are accurate. Descriptive words show the writer's opinions, yet they are fair. |
| sentence fluency | Sentences are complete. A variety of structures creates a pleasing rhythm. |
| conventions | Capitalization, spelling, punctuation, and grammar are correct. |

Below is the introduction to an editorial. In it, the writer identifies a debatable issue and states her position on the issue.

As our school district struggles to balance its budget, a disturbing question has come up: Which after-school sports could our district cancel in order to save money? Sports that may be cut include the girls' softball team and the boys' baseball team. The baseball field at each school would be rented out for community events during evenings, weekends, and summers. This may sound like a creative money-saving idea. But we students need to speak out against the idea that sports "cost too much." In a time when too many students are overweight, sports should be the last thing that our school wants to cut.

## Give It a Try: Examine the Model Paragraph

Working with a partner, use the model paragraph above to answer the following questions. Write your answers on separate paper.

1. **Ideas.**

   **a.** What is the hot topic that this writer has chosen to address?

   **b.** What is the writer's position on the issue?

2. **Organization.** Does the writer state her position in the beginning or at the end of the paragraph? Why do you think she chooses this location?

3. **Voice and word choice.** Which word in the first sentence tells you the writer's attitude toward the topic?

4. **Sentence fluency.** How does the writer use shorter and longer sentences?

5. **Conventions.** Explain the apostrophe rule used in the words *boys'* and *girls'*.

# Your Turn to Write: Compose an Editorial

Now it's your turn to write an editorial on a pressing topic. Read the assignment carefully and follow the strategies and instructions for each stage of the writing process.

## Assignment

What are some of the hot topics at your school? Choose a debatable issue that relates to your school and write an editorial of 300–350 words that

- identifies the issue
- states your position on the issue
- gives at least two reasons to support your opinion
- responds to one objection to your position
- concludes by restating your position

Your editorial should be suitable for publication in your school newspaper or other local paper.

## Prewrite

**Analyze the Prompt.** What does the prompt tell you about your goals for this assignment? Reread the assignment closely and answer the following questions. Write your answers on separate paper.

1. What is the purpose of this editorial?
2. Who is the audience for this editorial?
3. How long does the editorial need to be?

**Choose a Topic.**

1.  In a class discussion, make a list of at least five hot-topic issues at your school. Write them on your paper.

2.  Decide which topic on the lists interests you the most and circle it. This will be your topic for your editorial.

**Gather Ideas and Details.** As your teacher instructs, form a group with classmates who have chosen the same topic as you. As a group, identify two positions on the issue. Then brainstorm for reasons that support each position. Use the following T-chart to organize your work.

Topic: _____

| Position A: | Position B: |
|---|---|
| Supporting reasons: | Supporting reasons: |
| • | • |
| • | • |
| • | • |
| • | • |
| • | • |

Here is how one writer gathered ideas and details for an editorial on lending notebook computers to students.

Topic: the suggestion to set up a notebook computer-loan program at our library

| Position A: support the plan | Position B: oppose the plan |
|---|---|
| Supporting reasons: | Supporting reasons: |
| • some students don't own comp. | • too expensive |
| • useful software | • computer viruses |
| • public library has long wait lists | • damage to computers |
| • get homework more accurately and neatly | • these funds are needed for more important projects at school, such as classroom technology |
| • everyone should get to use a computer | |

**Organize Ideas and Details.** Now that you've gathered ideas about a hot topic at your school, plan how to organize your editorial. Filling in the following organizer will help you.

**Introduction:**

The issue: _____

My position on the issue: _____

My thesis statement: _____

**Body Paragraphs:**

My first supporting reason: _____

_____

My second (even stronger) supporting reason: _____

_____

My response to an opposing reason: _____

_____

**Conclusion:**

My restatement of my position on the issue: _____

_____

 Draft

Word choices are always important in a piece of writing, but they are especially important in persuasive writing. Your words can influence how your reader responds to your position. Using vivid, expressive words while remaining fair and polite will help you connect to your readers. On the other hand, using unfair descriptions or making fun of your opposition makes you seem overly emotional and unreliable.

**Use Expressive Yet Balanced Words.** The following table shows some ideas for choosing expressive yet balanced words. As you work on the draft of your editorial, add words to the boxes below.

| *When you want to defend an idea* | |
|---|---|
| fair | wise |
| clear | beneficial |
| obvious | |
| *When you want to criticize or find fault* | |
| unfounded | questionable |
| unlikely | unreasonable |
| doubtful | |

> *When you want to signal a contrast in ideas*
>
> on the other hand    in contrast
> in spite of          however
> despite that

**Write Your Editorial.** Using your prewriting and planning notes, write the rough draft of your editorial. Express your opinions confidently. Try to use fair, balanced words. However, if some words are overly emotional or unfair, you can replace them with balanced, fair words during the revision stage.

The model below shows how the writer made some changes to add fair, balanced words.

> Some people ~~stupidly~~ oppose the notebook–loan program.
> They ~~have the lame idea~~ *believe* that students will break the
> computers, lose them, or get viruses on them. However, these
> ~~extremists are~~ *opponents* ~~blind to~~ *overlooking* one fact. When a student checks
> a computer out, he or she signs a form, agreeing to be
> responsible for the computer. If the students loses or breaks
> the computer, he or she has to pay for the damage. For this
> reason, students will be very, very careful with this expensive
> equipment. ~~Duh! Problem solved.~~

 **Revise**

Use the following checklist to revise the rough draft of your editorial. The Editorial Rubric that follows the checklist will help you determine how strong your article is and where to make revisions.

### Ideas

❏ Underline the sentence(s) where you state a position on the issue. Revise the sentence if your position is not clear.

❏ Place a check mark next to each convincing reason and example you use. Cross out any reasons that are not convincing.

### Organization

❏ Make sure that your editorial has a beginning, a middle, and an end.

### Voice

❏ Do you show your concern or enthusiasm for your position on the issue while remaining fair and balanced? Write *voice* above the words or phrases that demonstrate your concern.

### Word choice

❏ Circle three vivid, expressive words.

❏ Circle three transitions you used to show contrasts.

### Sentence fluency

❏ Check that you used complete sentences.

❏ Check that you have sentence variety.

# Editorial Rubric

| | 4<br>Strong | 3<br>Effective | 2<br>Developing | 1<br>Beginning |
|---|---|---|---|---|
| **Ideas** | A clear position is supported with convincing reasons. | A clear position is stated, but reasons are not fully explained. | A position is stated and one reason is included. | The position is not clear. No specific reasons are included. |
| **organization** | Information is arranged logically, with a strong beginning, middle, and end. | Most information is arranged logically. There is a beginning, a middle, and an end. | Organization of information is awkward. The editorial needs a beginning or an end. | Information is included in no particular order. |
| **voice** | The writer uses a confident, balanced tone. | The writer's tone is mostly confident and balanced. | The writer uses a confident, balanced tone in one or two paragraphs. | The writer's tone is preachy, emotional, or otherwise unbalanced. |
| **word choice** | Words accurately and fairly help to express opinions. | A few words are inaccurate or unfair. | Many words are inaccurate or unfair. | Words do not accurately or fairly support opinions. |
| **sentence fluency** | Sentences are complete, and a variety of structures are used. | Sentences are mostly complete; some variety is used. | Most sentences are complete, but there is little variety. | Sentences are mostly incomplete or short and simple. |
| **conventions** | Few errors in capitalization, spelling, punctuation, or grammar are present. | Several errors in capitalization, spelling, punctuation, or grammar are present. | Errors in capitalization, spelling, punctuation, and grammar do not prevent understanding. | Errors in capitalization, spelling, punctuation, and grammar prevent understanding. |

## Edit

Now that you have revised your editorial, you are almost ready to publish it. One final step remains: editing the piece to correct mistakes in capitalization, spelling, punctuation, or grammar. When you check the grammar in your editorial, check for subject-verb agreement. The following mini-lesson explains how.

## Mini-Lesson: Making Subjects and Verbs Agree

As you know, a noun or pronoun can be singular or plural.
Singular: computer, student, person, he, she
Plural: computers, students, people, they

When you use a singular noun or pronoun as the subject of a sentence, it forms a singular subject. Likewise, when you use a plural noun or pronoun as the subject of a sentence, it forms a plural subject.

→ A **subject** is the word or word group that performs an action or state of being in a sentence.

This computer has a word-processing program on it.

These computers are available for checkout.

→ A **verb** is the word or word group that expresses action or links the subject to another word in the sentence.

This computer has a word-processing program on it.

These computers are available for checkout.

In a sentence, the verb must *agree* with its subject. This means that if the subject is singular, then the verb must be singular, too.

One student <u>needs</u> to borrow a notebook computer.

He <u>wants</u> it right away.

Likewise, if the subject is plural, the verb must be plural.

Five students <u>need</u> to borrow notebook computers.

They <u>want</u> them right away.

## Give It a Try: Edit for Subject-Verb Agreement

In each of the following sentences, underline the subject once and the verb twice. If the subject and verb agree, write *Agree* on the blank line. If the subject and verb do not agree, cross out the verb and write the correct form of the verb above it.

*Examples:* _____*Agree*_____ **a.** The <u>mouse</u> for the computer <u>connects</u> to this port.

_____ **b.** <u>Computers</u> for the loan program ~~has~~ *have* <u>arrived</u>.

_____ **1.** We like the idea of a computer-loan program.

_____ **2.** These volunteers has computer experience.

_____ **3.** This power cord belong with that computer.

_____ **4.** A waiting list for the computers has formed already.

_____ **5.** Roger, the redheaded boy, know about software installation.

## Give It a Try: Edit Your Editorial for Subject-Verb Agreement

Read the draft of your editorial carefully, noticing the subject and verb in each sentence. If it helps, underline each subject once and each verb twice, or draw an arrow from the subject to the verb. If a verb does not agree with its subject, make a correction to create subject-verb agreement.

**Edit Your Editorial.** Edit the revised copy of your editorial. The following questions will help you decide what to change, remove, or leave in place.

**Conventions**
- ❏  Does each verb agree with its subject?
- ❏  Did you capitalize proper nouns?
- ❏  Did you use commas to separate words, phrases, or clauses in a series?
- ❏  Did you use a comma when you joined sentences with a co-ordinating conjunction?
- ❏  Did you use a comma when you began a sentence with an introductory element?
- ❏  Did you correct punctuation errors, either with a friend's help or by using a handbook?
- ❏  Did you correct spelling mistakes, either with a friend's help or by using a dictionary?
- ❏  Did you correct grammar mistakes, either with a friend's help or by using a grammar handbook?

### PUBLISH

**Presentation.** Prepare your editorial for publication by writing or typing the final, edited copy.

**Publish Your Editorial.** Here are ideas for publishing your editorial.

- ❑ Submit the editorial for publication in your school newspaper.
- ❑ If your school has a Web page where students can post opinion pieces, post your editorial there.
- ❑ If you have a blog, post the editorial as an entry.
- ❑ Give a copy of your editorial to someone who shares your interest in the issue. This person could be a classmate, a teacher, or even a family member.
- ❑ Give a copy of your editorial to someone who opposes your viewpoint. After he or she has read your editorial, have a discussion about your different views on the issue.

## Evaluate Your Editorial

Your teacher will either assess your editorial, ask you to self-assess your editorial, or ask you to switch with a partner and assess each other's work.

## Evaluate the Model Editorial

Work with a partner to evaluate the model editorial that follows. Use the rubric on page 139 and write your score here: _____. In a class discussion, explain the score that you gave.

### The Notebook Loan Idea

Imagine being able to go to our school library and check out a notebook computer to take home. You could use the word-processing software to prepare an essay, or you could use a spreadsheet program for a math project. You wouldn't have to waste time trekking to a public library, only to wait in line for a computer that you can use only for 45 minutes. Some opponents point out that it would be expensive to buy all those computers and software licenses. They say students will break the notebooks and get computer viruses on them. Despite these objections, making notebook computers available for checkout is the only responsible choice.

One reason why the notebook-loan program is responsible is that it gives all students equal access to current technology. Not all students have computers at home. If our school wants to educate all students equally, then it needs to make sure all students have the opportunity to work on a computer. Each student needs to learn to type, use a word-processing program, and use spreadsheets. It is irresponsible to say, "If you don't own a computer, too bad. You'll just have to miss out on that part of education."

Another reason why the program is responsible is that it gives students a chance to excel. A lot of our learning takes place out of class, when we write reports and essays and do homework. A notebook has the tools to help us produce better work. For example, a word-processing program can help you check your spelling and grammar. It can also make your work perfectly readable, as opposed to your best (but still unreadable) handwriting.

Some people oppose the notebook-loan program. They believe that students will break the computers, lose them, or get viruses on them. However, these opponents are overlooking one fact. When a student checks a computer out, he or she signs a form, agreeing to be responsible for the computer. If the students loses or breaks the computer, he or she has to pay for the damage. For this reason, students will be very, very careful with this expensive equipment.

Despite objections, the idea to start up a notebook-loan program is the responsible thing to do for students at this school. It will teach equality, technology, and responsibility. The school has a responsibility to its students to provide the best education possible, and this is one step toward accomplishing that goal.

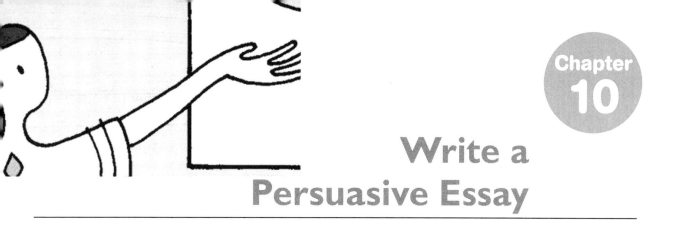

# Write a Persuasive Essay

In Chapter 9, you learned about the editorial. In this chapter, you'll learn about the persuasive essay. Both types of writing persuade readers to agree with the writer's opinions or to take a certain action. But the two types of persuasive writing are different, too.

Editorials are written about a current hot topic of interest to newspaper or magazine readers. **Persuasive essays**, on the other hand, may be written about a broader selection of debatable topics. The topics may be related to a school class, your personal life, events in the news, athletic training techniques—the list is practically endless.

As you work through the process of writing a persuasive essay in this chapter, you will build upon what you learned about writing editorials.

## Six Traits of a **Persuasive Essay**

| | |
|---|---|
| **Ideas** | The writer has a specific persuasive purpose (reason for writing). Reasons and examples support the purpose. |
| **organization** | The introduction states the writer's purpose. Body paragraphs give supporting reasons. The conclusion restates the purpose. |
| **voice** | The writer's enthusiasm or concern for the topic causes the reader to consider the persuasive purpose carefully. |
| **word choice** | Subject-area words or terms are used accurately and help to achieve the purpose for writing. |
| **sentence fluency** | Sentences are complete. A variety of structures creates a pleasing rhythm. |
| **conventions** | Capitalization, spelling, punctuation, and grammar are correct. |

In the persuasive paragraph below, the writer tries to convince readers to make an earth-friendly change in their habits at home.

One of the most wasteful habits of the modern household is the use of paper towels and napkins. They waste Earth's resources, and they waste your family's money. Consequently, you should replace these products with an earth-friendly alternative: reusable towels and napkins. This solution is simple and will not cost you any extra money. Here's what to do. The next time you need to buy paper towels and napkins, buy a stack of small towels and cloth napkins instead. Put these out in the kitchen and at the dining table. Now, simply launder the soiled cloths along with your other laundry. Since they are reusable, you will not have to keep buying them week after week, year after year. You have instantly increased your savings and decreased your household garbage.

## Give It a Try: Examine the Model Paragraph

Use the model paragraph above to complete the following steps. Then, in a class discussion, explain your responses.

1. **Ideas.** Copy the sentence that expresses the writer's main idea.
2. **Organization.** Copy the sentence that forms the conclusion of the paragraph.
3. **Voice and word choice.** The writer uses the second-person point of view. Why do you think she does this?
4. **Sentence fluency.** Which sentence is a compound sentence? Copy it and circle the comma and coordinating conjunction.
5. **Conventions.** Why does the writer use a colon in the third sentence?

# Your Turn to Write: Compose a Persuasive Essay

Now it's your turn to write a convincing essay. Read the assignment carefully and follow the strategies and instructions for each stage of the writing process.

## Assignment

Beginning next semester, your school will offer two different Green Electives per semester. A Green Elective will teach a skill that helps students use Earth's resources responsibly. A committee of teachers must choose which two electives to offer first. Here are a few courses they are considering:

Gardening and Composting

Furniture Construction and Repair

Fashion Design and Sewing

Cooking Healthy Family Meals

Write a 400-word essay in which you persuade the committee to offer the Green Elective of your choice. It can be a topic from the list above or another one that you choose.

## Prewrite

**Analyze the Prompt.** What does the prompt tell you about your goals for this assignment? Reread the assignment closely and answer the following questions. Write your answers on separate paper.

1. What is the purpose of this essay?
2. Who is the audience for this essay?
3. How long does the essay need to be?

**Choose a Topic.** With your teacher's permission, gather in a small group.

1. With group members, discuss your ideas about the Green Elective's topics. In your opinion, which elective is most likely to help students use Earth's resources responsibly? Explain your point of view.

2. After the group discussion, complete the following sentence by writing on the lines provided. You are identifying the topic for your persuasive essay.

I think that the electives committee should offer _____

_____ Green Elective because_____

_____

**Gather Ideas and Details.** Now that you've chosen a specific topic, explore that topic further to gather ideas and details for your essay. With your teacher's permission, gather in a small group of students who are writing about the same topic. Discuss your ideas about what makes this elective a good choice for a Green Elective. To get the discussion going, use these sentence starters:

This skill can be considered a "green skill" because . . .

Basically, this class would teach students to . . .

This skill is especially important because . . .

A question I have about this skill is . . .

I used the skill one time when I . . .

This skill/class is *not* . . .

**Organize Ideas and Details.** You can use a persuasive map to record your purpose for writing and the supporting reasons and details. Review the information you collected during the group discussion and fill in the persuasive map on the next page.

| My purpose for writing is to | | |
|---|---|---|

↓

| Reason 1: | | |
|---|---|---|
| Detail: | Detail: | Detail: |

↓

| Reason 2: | | |
|---|---|---|
| Detail: | Detail: | Detail: |

↓

| Reason 3: | | |
|---|---|---|
| Detail: | Detail: | Detail: |

In the following model, the writer has organized ideas about a Gardening and Composting class.

**My purpose for writing is to** convince the electives committee to offer Gardening and Composting as a Green Elective.

↓

**Reason 1:** Gardening and composting are easy to learn.

| Detail: | Detail: | Detail: |
|---|---|---|
| any student has the skill to do it | need teacher to explain how to do it and help with problems | |

↓

**Reason 2:** Gardening can be done by any student, in an apartment or a house with a yard.

| Detail: | Detail: | Detail: |
|---|---|---|
| flowerpots on porch or balcony | share a garden in one person's yard | use a relative's yard |

↓

**Reason 3:** Composting is important, but most students need a teacher to explain how and where to build a compost heap

| Detail: | Detail: | Detail: |
|---|---|---|
| Can the school set up compost bins on school property? | Can home-compost materials be donated to a local farm? | Can composting be done in a large flowerpot? |

As you know, a strong introductory paragraph contains a thesis statement. (You can review the mini-lesson on writing a thesis statement on page 89.) In a persuasive essay, the thesis statement declares exactly what the writer wants the reader to agree with, believe, or do.

Here are examples of thesis statements from the models in this chapter.

*Consequently, you should replace these products with an earth-friendly alternative: reusable towels and napkins.*

(This thesis statement identifies a clear persuasive purpose for writing the paragraph.)

*Therefore, it is urgent that the electives committee approve Gardening and Composting as one of the two Green Electives that the school will offer.*

(This thesis statement states *who* should do *what*. The body of the essay will give supporting reasons and examples.)

**Write a Thesis Statement.** On separate paper, write a thesis statement for your persuasive essay.

Just as the introductory paragraph needs a strong thesis statement, other paragraphs need strong topic sentences. The following mini-lesson will help you write clear, effective topic sentences for your paragraphs.

## Mini-Lesson: Writing Topic Sentences

As you know, each paragraph in an essay develops one main idea to support or explain the essay's thesis. The sentence that expresses the main idea of a paragraph is a *topic sentence*.

→ A **topic sentence** expresses the main idea of a paragraph. The other sentences in the paragraph give details, examples, facts, or other support.

In the following model paragraph, the topic sentence is underlined. The remaining sentences give supporting details.

<u>Gardening is a realistic goal for any student, even those who live in apartments.</u> Many vegetables can be grown in large flowerpots on a porch or balcony. In addition, students can team up and grow a garden in one person's yard. My uncle, for instance, has a large yard that he would let me and a friend grow a garden in. At home in my apartment, I could grow carrots, radishes, tomatoes, onions, and herbs in pots.

Each topic sentence in an essay expresses a key reason or idea of the essay. In a persuasive essay, a topic sentence expresses one reason why the reader should agree with the thesis.

## Give It a Try: Write a Topic Sentence

The following paragraph is missing a topic sentence. On the line provided, write a topic sentence that expresses the main idea of the paragraph.

_____

_____ For this reason, we need a class to teach us how and where to compost. For instance, can the school set up compost bins on school property? Is there a local farmer who would take donations for the farm's compost heap? Can compost heaps be created in a large flowerpot, like gardens can? Students need someone to answer these questions.

## Give It a Try: Write Topic Sentences for Your Paragraphs

Look at the persuasive map that you created on page 149. Each block of a Reason plus Details represents one paragraph in the body of your essay. Use the information in each Reason box to write a topic sentence that expresses the main idea of that paragraph. Write your topic sentences on separate paper.

**Write Your Persuasive Essay.** It's time to write the rough draft of your persuasive essay. Use your persuasive map, your thesis statement, and your topic sentences to compose a well-organized and well-supported essay.

## Revise

You have put a lot of planning, organization, and written work into the creation of your essay. You have written a complete draft of the essay. Now step back and look at the big picture by getting some gut-level responses from fellow writers.

**Get Peer Feedback.** Gather in a circle of four to five classmates, as your teacher directs. Pass a clean copy of your rough draft to the person sitting on your left. Each person should read silently. Then take turns sharing reactions to one another's writing. Use the following sentence starters:

Something I liked about this essay is . . .

Something that I wanted to know more about is . . .

I think the target audience would be persuaded because . . .

I think the target audience would want to know more about . . .

As you listen to feedback on your essay, take notes. Do you need to explain a reason in greater detail? Add a supporting reason?

**Revise Your Persuasive Essay.** Make necessary revisions to the content or organization of your essay. Use the peer feedback you received, along with the following checklist. The Persuasive Writing Rubric that follows the checklist will help you determine how strong your essay is and where to make revisions.

### Ideas

❑ Place a check mark above the sentence where you state a clear persuasive purpose for writing.

❑ Underline three convincing reasons and examples. Revise or remove any reasons that are weak.

### Organization

❑ Make sure that your essay has a beginning, a middle, and an end.

❑ Check that each paragraph has a topic sentence.

❑ Remove any ideas or details that stray from the topic of each paragraph.

### Voice

❑ Find three words that show your enthusiasm for your topic. Write *voice* above them.

### Word choice

❑ Check that you used specialized words or terms accurately.

### Sentence fluency

❑ Check that you used complete sentences.

❑ Check for sentence variety. Revise sentence structures and sentence lengths if necessary.

# Persuasive Essay Rubric

| | 4<br>Strong | 3<br>Effective | 2<br>Developing | 1<br>Beginning |
|---|---|---|---|---|
| **Ideas** | The essay has a clear persuasive purpose and convincing reasons. | A clear purpose is stated, but reasons are not fully explained. | The purpose or the reasons may be unfocused or only loosely connected. | The purpose is not clear. No specific reasons are included. |
| **organization** | Information is arranged logically, with a strong beginning, a middle, and an end. | Most information is arranged logically. | Organization of information is awkward. | Information is included in random order. |
| **voice** | The writer uses a confident, engaging tone. | The writer's tone is mostly confident and engaging. | The writer uses a confident, engaging tone in one or two paragraphs. | The writer's tone is flat, dull, or uncaring. |
| **word choice** | Specialized words or terms are used accurately. | Most specialized words or terms are used accurately. | Specialized words are used, but many are used inaccurately. | No specialized words or terms are used accurately. |
| **sentence fluency** | Sentences are complete, and a variety of structures are used. | Sentences are mostly complete; some variety is used. | Most sentences are complete, but there is little variety. | Sentences are mostly incomplete or short and simple. |
| **conventions** | Few errors in capitalization, spelling, punctuation, or grammar are present. | Several errors in capitalization, spelling, punctuation, or grammar are present. | Errors in capitalization, spelling, punctuation, and grammar do not prevent understanding. | Errors in capitalization, spelling, punctuation, and grammar prevent understanding. |

## Edit

Edit the revised copy of your persuasive essay. The following questions will help you decide what to change, remove, or leave in place.

### Conventions
- ❑ Does each verb agree with its subject?
- ❑ Did you use commas to separate words, phrases, or clauses in a series?
- ❑ Did you use a comma when you joined sentences with a coordinating conjunction?
- ❑ Did you use a comma when you began a sentence with an introductory element?
- ❑ Did you correct punctuation errors, either with a friend's help or by using a handbook?
- ❑ Did you correct spelling mistakes, either with a friend's help or by using a dictionary?
- ❑ Did you correct grammar mistakes, either with a friend's help or by using a grammar handbook?

## PUBLISH

**Presentation.** Prepare your essay for publication by writing or typing the final, edited copy.

**Publish Your Essay.** Here are some ideas for publishing your persuasive essay.
- ❑ Share your essay with someone who may be able to teach you the skill you wrote about, or who may be interested in learning the skill with you.
- ❑ Write a letter to your principal, persuading him or her to offer Green Electives at your school. Include a copy of your essay to demonstrate what you have in mind.
- ❑ Share your essay with a friend who knows very little about the topic you wrote about. Then answer any questions he or she has about the topic.

# Evaluate Your Essay

Your teacher will either assess your essay, ask you to self-assess your essay, or ask you to switch with a partner and assess each other's work.

## Evaluate the Model Persuasive Essay.

Work with a partner to evaluate the following model essay. Use the rubric on page 155 and write your score here: _____. In a class discussion, explain the score that you gave.

### Going Green by Growing Green

World leaders are speaking out about global warming. Scientists are begging people to help save the rain forests for the good of Earth. Community leaders are asking residents to reduce, reuse, and recycle. And what does our school ask of its students? Nothing. Our school does not offer one single class on how students can help protect Earth. Therefore, it is urgent that the electives committee approve Gardening and Composting as one of the two Green Electives that the school will offer.

Gardening and composting are not hard skills to learn, so it would make an excellent choice for the Green Electives program. Any student can take this course and make earth-saving changes right away. But no matter how easy it may be to grow a garden and start a compost heap, someone needs to teach students how to get started.

Gardening is a realistic goal for any student, even those who live in apartments. Many vegetables can be grown in large flowerpots on a porch or balcony. In addition, students can team up and grow a garden in one person's yard. My uncle, for instance, has a large yard that he would let me and a friend grow a garden in. At home in my apartment, I could grow carrots, radishes, tomatoes, onions, and herbs in pots. Before I could do any of this, however, I would need to learn how.

Composting is an important green skill, but finding a place to build a compost heap may be a challenge for many students. For this reason, we need a class to teach us how and where to compost. For instance, can the school set up compost bins on school property? Is there a local farmer who would take donations for the farm's compost heap? Can compost heaps be created in a large flowerpot, like gardens can? Students need someone to answer these questions.

Above all, gardening and composting will help students learn how to use what little land they have to produce their own food. Growing a home garden saves money on groceries. It also saves fuel because the produce doesn't have to be delivered to a store, and you don't have to drive there to buy it and bring it home. Home gardens can help heal our world, and students need to know how we can start this important activity.

# Write a
# Persuasive Brochure

A *persuasive brochure* is a short folded document whose purpose is to persuade readers to buy a product or service.

**Mini-Glossary: Brochures**

**brochure**  A folded paper containing persuasive or informational content.

**panel**  One "page" of a brochure, after it has been folded.

**bi-fold brochure**  A four-panel brochure formed by folding a sheet of paper in half.

**tri-fold brochure**  A six-panel brochure formed by folding a sheet of paper in thirds.

**white space**  The part of the page that has no print or images on it.

In this chapter, you will learn how you can use your skills of persuasive writing to create a persuasive brochure.

## Six Traits of a Persuasive Brochure

| Ideas | The brochure has one specific persuasive purpose. |
|---|---|
| organization | Information is organized in a logical way, such as from most to least important. |
| voice | The writer's tone fits with the persuasive purpose and the target audience. |
| word choice | Vivid words help to make the writer's ideas clear. |
| sentence fluency | Sentences are short and clear. Incomplete sentences are clear in meaning. |
| conventions | Capitalization, spelling, punctuation, and grammar are correct. |

The model below shows the front cover of a trifold brochure. Read the brochure cover and then complete the activity that follows.

Camille's
Pet-Sitting Services

Loving care for your pet
when you are away

Camille Henderson
experienced pet caregiver
(212) 555-4837
chenderson@mail.com

## Give It a Try: Examine the Model Brochure

Use the model brochure cover on the left to answer the following questions. Write your answers on separate paper.

1. **Ideas.** What service is this brochure selling?
2. **Organization.** What kinds of persuasive tactics or arguments does the author use? (You'll learn more about persuasive techniques later in this chapter.)
3. **Voice and word choice.** List two words from the brochure cover that helped you answer item 2.
4. **Sentence fluency.** Why do you think the writer uses short word groups instead of paragraphs?
5. **Conventions.** Why do you think the writer uses an incomplete sentence?

## Your Turn to Write: Create a Persuasive Brochure

Now it's your turn to create a convincing brochure. Read the assignment carefully and follow the strategies and instructions for each stage of the writing process.

# Assignment

Some extra cash in your pocket is always welcome. Do you have a talent or skill that you could turn into a valuable service to sell? Here are a few ideas.

reading or math coach            leatherworker
babysitter                       small chores expert
pet sitter or dog walker         baker
yard worker                      house cleaner
closet organizer                 greeting card maker

Choose a job description, either from the list above or from your own experience, and write a tri-fold brochure to persuade people to buy your service. Write your brochure using a specific sales technique, and include drawings or pictures to illustrate your ideas.

## Prewrite

**Analyze the Prompt.** What does the prompt tell you about your goals for this assignment? Read the assignment closely to find answers to the following questions. Write your answers on separate paper.

1.  What is the purpose of this brochure?
2.  Who is the audience for this brochure?
3.  What is the brochure's format?

**Choose a Topic.** Review the list of possible topics in the writing assignment. Next to the printed list of topics, write additional ideas you have. Finally, choose one of these topics for your brochure and circle it.

**Gather Ideas and Details.** Gather information to include in your brochure by writing details in the table on the next page. You may find it helpful to research your topic in how-to books or how-to Internet pages.

**Brochure topic:** _____

| What I can do for my clients: | My experience (why I am good at this): |
|---|---|
| Details of my service or product: | Ideas for drawings or pictures for the brochure: |
| My fees/prices and when I can work: | How to contact me: |
| Additional notes: | |

**Organize Ideas and Details.** The ideas and images in your brochure will support a single *persuasive strategy*, or method of persuading people to pay for your services. Before you gather ideas and details for your brochure, you will need to decide which persuasive strategy to use. The following mini-lesson explains different types of persuasive strategies.

# Mini-Lesson: Persuasive Strategies

A *persuasive strategy* is a way of convincing readers to take an action or agree with an idea. Following are some commonly used strategies.

## Persuasive Strategies

| | |
|---|---|
| **Appeal to Logic** | The writer uses evidence, statistics, or scientific data to convince the reader. *My clients' math scores improve a full letter grade after only five of my coaching sessions.* |
| **Appeal to Emotion** | The writer uses words and ideas that create an emotional response in order to convince the reader. *Imagine the comfort of coming home to a clean, fresh-smelling house.* |
| **Humorous Approach** | The writer uses funny ideas and images to convince the reader. *Tired of stepping in dog poo in your yard? It's time to call a cleanup expert!* |
| **Testimonial** | The writer uses a quotation from a satisfied client to convince the reader. *"Alex's hand-tooled leather belts are the most popular gift I gave to my friends last holiday season."—Anne McCord, Los Angeles, CA* |
| **Bandwagon** | The writer paints a picture of "everybody" using the service or product to convince the reader to "jump on the bandwagon." *Eight out of ten households in your apartment building use my babysitting services.* |
| **Plain Folks** | The writer paints a picture of normal, everyday people using the product or service. *Like working moms across the city, you probably need a little help around the house. That's where I come in.* |
| **Snob Appeal** | The writer paints a picture of wealthy or glamorous people using the product or service. *Women with the best taste give only the best greeting cards: those crafted by hand.* |

## Give It a Try: Identify Persuasive Strategies

Decide which persuasive strategy each of the following examples uses. On separate paper, write the name of the strategy. In a class discussion, explain your answers.

1. Experience relaxation and happiness by letting me organize your closets.
2. Is grammar holding you hostage? Break free! Hire me as your personal grammar coach.
3. Ninety percent of people who buy my homemade cookies call me again to buy more.
4. Down-to-earth leather wallets, handmade for down-to-earth people like you.
5. Don't be the only one giving impersonal store-bought cards. Order personalized handmade cards from me today!
6. Top community leaders have a secret: They save valuable time by hiring out their housework.
7. "I wasn't sure about asking a teenager to watch my toddler, but Stephanie proved to be trustworthy, fun, and caring."—Tracy, mother of a 2-year-old girl
8. Only a cat lover could know how to keep your precious cat safe and loved while you're away.
9. The fallen autumn leaves in your yard are biodegradable. Hire me to rake and bag them in 100% biodegradable bags.
10. Your garage called. It's down in the dumps. Call the Garage Doctor to clean it up!

## Give It a Try: Choose a Persuasive Strategy for Your Brochure

On separate paper, answer each of the following questions.

1. Which persuasive strategy best fits with the purpose and audience of your brochure?
2. Write one example of how you can use this strategy to convince your readers to use your service.

**Organize the Brochure.** Plan how to arrange information in your persuasive brochure. Start by folding a sheet of paper into a trifold brochure. On each panel, identify or list the information and artwork for that section. Be sure to make choices that support the brochure's persuasive strategy. Keep the following tips in mind:

### The Cover

- Use the cover to hook readers' interest so they want to open the brochure and read more.
- Include a graphic (drawing, etc.) and plenty of white space on the cover.

### The Inside Panels

- Use the inside panels to give information about your services.
- Group information by topic (the specific tasks you do, descriptions of products, pay rates, etc.) with clear section titles.
- Arrange information from most to least important. This way, even if the reader looks at only the first panel, he or she will read your most important points.
- Use organizational aides such as bullets, arrows, check marks, question marks, etc. Pick one type and stick to it.
- Use enough white space so that each panel isn't overcrowded.

### The Back Panels

- The back panel that folds into the brochure is actually the *first* panel that readers see when they open the brochure. Use this panel to give an overview of your service, to describe your experience, or to give other high-priority information.
- Use the center back panel to restate your persuasive purpose, to give testimonials (even if the testimonial is not your persuasive strategy), or to showcase a useful graphic.

**T!p**   You don't have to be an artist—your computer is! It has hundreds of pictures you can use. Go to the Insert menu and click on Symbol. You will find symbols, webdings, and wingdings. To add one of them, put your cursor where you want to insert the picture, highlight the picture on the symbol page, and click Insert. You can make these bigger by changing the font size. You can color them, too. And of course you can make some type **boldface** or <u>underlined</u> or in CAPITALS.

## Draft

Use the rough plan to create a full draft version of the brochure. Write the text for each panel. You can use neat handwriting or typed copy that you cut and paste on the blank brochure. Here are some tips:

- Keep sentences and paragraphs short.
- Sentence fragments are okay, as long as their meaning is clear.
- Use plenty of white space on each panel.
- Organize information logically.
- Include drawings or other images to illustrate your ideas. Create your own images or clip them out of magazines.

## Revise

Now that you have laid out a complete copy of your brochure, examine it closely. Read the text. Stand back and look at the appearance of the brochure (the combination of text, images, and white space). Answer the following questions and make changes if necessary.

## Ideas
- ❑ Does the brochure express one persuasive purpose?
- ❑ Are supporting reasons and examples convincing?
- ❑ Do you provide contact information?

## Organization
- ❑ Does the cover of the brochure hook the reader's interest?
- ❑ Do the inside panels give relevant information in a logical order?
- ❑ Does the back panel restate the brochure's persuasive purpose?
- ❑ Do images and white space help to create a pleasing appearance? Remove any clutter, or add images if necessary.

## Voice
- ❑ Do you use a tone that fits with your target audience? Write *voice* above three words or phrases that demonstrate this tone.

## Word choice
- ❑ Circle three vivid, accurate words you used to make your ideas clear. Revise any inaccurate or confusing words.

## Sentence fluency
- ❑ Revise any sentences that are too long.
- ❑ If you used incomplete sentences, are their meanings clear?

# Rubric for a **Persuasive Brochure**

| | 4 Strong | 3 Effective | 2 Developing | 1 Beginning |
|---|---|---|---|---|
| **Ideas** | A specific service is marketed with convincing details. | A service is marketed. Most details are convincing. | A service is described, but details are not persuasive. | No specific service is marketed. |
| **organization** | The cover hooks the reader's interest. Information is arranged logically. | The cover identifies the service. Most information is arranged logically. | The cover does not make the service clear. Organization of information is awkward. | The brochure needs a cover. Information is included in no particular order. |
| **voice** | The writer's tone fits with the persuasive strategy and the audience. | On most panels, the tone fits with the persuasive strategy and audience. | On a few panels, the tone fits with the persuasive strategy or audience. | The tone does not fit with the persuasive strategy or the audience. |
| **word choice** | Vivid words make ideas clear on each panel. | Vivid words make ideas clear on most panels. | Vivid words make ideas clear on a few panels. | Vocabulary is weak, inaccurate, or confusing. |
| **sentence fluency** | Each sentence and word group has a clear meaning. | Most sentences and word groups have a clear meaning. | Many sentences or word groups have unclear or incomplete meanings. | Most sentences or word groups are confusing or inaccurate. |
| **conventions** | Capitalization, spelling, punctuation, and grammar are correct. | A few errors in capitalization, spelling, punctuation, or grammar are present. | Errors in conventions do not prevent understanding of the brochure. | Errors in conventions make it hard to understand the brochure. |

## Edit

Edit the revised copy of your brochure to correct mistakes in capitalization, spelling, punctuation, and grammar.

### PUBLISH

**Presentation.** Based on the edited draft of the brochure, prepare a final copy for publication. Fold the paper crisply. Use neat handwriting in black ink, or cut and paste typed copy. Carefully glue images in place.

**Publish Your Brochure.** Here are ideas for publishing your brochure.

- ❏ Display your brochure on a bulletin board in class.
- ❏ At a photocopy center, make copies of your brochure to give to your target audience. (Be sure to get a parent or guardian's permission first.)

## Evaluate Your Brochure

Your teacher will either assess your brochure, ask you to self-assess your brochure, or ask you to switch with a partner and assess each other's work.

## Evaluate a Model Persuasive Brochure

Work with a partner to evaluate the following model brochure. Use the rubric on page 168 and write your score here: _____. In a class discussion, explain the score that you gave.

## Qualifications

I have a Junior Volunteer certification from Homeward Bound Pet Shelter.

### Experience

Two years' experience, including dogs, cats, rats, mice, hamsters, gerbils, ferrets, and birds. I love them all!

inward-folding back panel

# *Camille's*

## Pet-Sitting Services

 Loving

 Educated

 Reliable

Camille Henderson

(212) 555-4837

chenderson@mail.com

center back panel

# *Camille's*

## Pet-Sitting Services

*Loving care for your pet when you are away*

Camille Henderson

experienced pet caregiver

(212) 555-4837

chenderson@mail.com

front panel

## Why Hire a Pro?

As a trained pet sitter, I am not only loving and gentle, but I am educated. I can handle

- emergencies
- medications
- feeding
- grooming
- cleanup
- play

## When I Can Work

- Monday–Friday after 4:00 P.M.
- Saturday and Sunday between 9:00 A.M. and 4:00 P.M.

## My Rates

$5 per half hour
$10 per hour

## Transportation

Reliable transportation provided by my loving mom!

## Testimonials

"A true professional!"
—Helen Garrett, dog owner

"My two cats love it when Camille visits. They are always relaxed and happy afterward."
—Peter Slone, cat owner

"Camille follows my instructions to the letter. Thank you, Camille!"
—Debbie, owner of two cats and one dog

left inner panel          center inner panel          right inner panel

# Test Writing:
# The Persuasive Essay

If a friend in another city told you that his school has a no-home-work policy, what would you think? Would you envy him? Or would you wonder how he has time to master all the lessons? Some schools assign lots of homework, while other schools assign little or none. The topic of homework is *debatable*, meaning that people have very different opinions about it.

Thinking and writing about debatable topics helps you prepare to write strong persuasive responses on tests. As with any test essay, a persuasive essay allows you to show how well you can use the traits of writing. In addition, by stating and defending your opinion, you demonstrate your *critical-thinking* skills—your ability to use reason and logic. This chapter will help you prepare to show off your writing and thinking skills on a persuasive writing test.

## Six Traits of a Persuasive Test Essay

| | |
|---|---|
| **Ideas** | The topic is narrowed to a specific position to be defended. Reasons and examples support the position. |
| **Organization** | The introduction states the writer's position. Body paragraphs give supporting reasons and respond to objections. The conclusion restates the position. |
| **Voice** | The writer's voice shows concern or enthusiasm, balanced with a sense of trustworthiness. |
| **Word Choice** | Words are accurate and fair. |
| **Sentence Fluency** | Sentences are complete. A variety of structures creates a pleasing rhythm. |
| **Conventions** | Capitalization, spelling, punctuation, and grammar are correct. |

# Preparing to Write Your Test Essay

A persuasive writing prompt will give you a topic and ask you to take a side or express an opinion. Here is an example of this kind of prompt.

---

**Instructions**

You have 55 minutes to complete the written composition. Read the prompt below. Then use separate paper to plan and draft your composition. Only your draft will be scored.

**Writing Prompt**

Some researchers say that doing homework helps students learn and remember better. Others say that homework doesn't improve performance and takes away from family time. What do you think? Write an essay for your principal to read. Explain whether you think homework is a necessary or an unnecessary part of learning at your school.

**Remember to**

- write about the assigned topic
- state a clear opinion on the topic
- use convincing reasons and examples
- respond to at least one objection to your viewpoint
- edit your writing to correct mistakes in conventions

---

## 1. Study the Prompt

Before you begin to write your essay, take a few moments to study the prompt. Answer these important questions:

**What is the purpose of the essay?** Scan the prompt for key words that tell you what kind of essay to write.

**Words That Signal a Persuasive Essay**

| | |
|---|---|
| opinion | perspective |
| point of view | whether or not |
| reasons | agree/disagree |

**What should you write about?** A writing prompt includes two or three main parts. The context, or setup, gives you background information on the topic. In the prompt on page 174, the setup is the first paragraph.

A prompt also includes a specific, focused writing assignment. In the prompt on page 174, the writing task is this:

*Write an essay for your principal to read. Explain whether you think homework is a necessary or an unnecessary part of learning at your school.*

A writing prompt often—but not always—includes reminders about what to include. In the prompt on page 174, the reminders are included last, in a bullet list. Don't skip over this section! Read the list carefully to learn what teachers will look for when they score your essay test.

**How much time do you have to write?** The prompt states that students have 55 minutes to write their essays. If a prompt does not state a time limit, look for the information on another page in your test booklet or ask your teacher.

## 2. Plan Your Time
After studying the prompt, make a quick plan for how to use your time. If you have 55 minutes to write the essay, you could use your time as follows:

| 15 minutes: | Study the prompt and complete the prewriting. |
| 25 minutes: | Write the essay. |
| 10 minutes: | Revise the essay. Make "big" changes now, such as adding or removing sentences, moving sentences, and clarifying sentences. |
| 5 minutes: | Edit the essay. Fix mistakes in capitalization, spelling, punctuation, and grammar. |

## 3. Prewrite
During the time set aside for prewriting, decide your opinion on the topic, gather ideas and details, and organize the information.

**Take a stand on the issue.** Remember that there is no "correct" opinion to have. Rather, your essay will be scored on how well you support the opinion you express. Use a few minutes of prewriting time to decide which point of view you can best support. A T-chart or pro-con chart, like the one below, can help.

**Gather ideas and details.** A T-chart or pro-con chart not only helps you decide your opinion on the issue. It also helps you gather supporting reasons, examples, and facts. Look at the pro-con chart below. Based on the ideas listed in each side, which side of the issue would you take?

TOOLKIT

For a persuasive essay, useful prewriting strategies include
- T-chart
- pro-con chart
- listing
- freewriting

homework

| pros | cons |
|---|---|
| extra time to practice new material | too hard to learn new material on my own |
| time to work at my own pace | too much homework to get done each night |
| a way to show my parents what I do in school | takes away from time I could spend with my family |
| a reason to learn how to manage my time | just repeats stuff from class; boring |
| helps me learn to take charge of my time | encourages people to copy each other's work |
| helps me learn to make myself do things I should do but don't want to do | takes away time that should be spent on sports, hobbies, family time |

**Organize the information.** Use your remaining prewriting time to plan the arrangement of information in your essay. During a 55-minute testing period, it is reasonable to plan for a 4- to 6-paragraph essay. Use a simple strategy to organize the introduction, body, and conclusion of the essay.

In a persuasive essay, it works well to arrange your reasons from least to most important. That way, you end on a strong note. Include your response to an objection in the paragraph about one of your reasons, or in a separate paragraph before your final, strongest reason.

> TOOLKIT
>
> For a persuasive essay, useful organizing strategies include
> - beginning-middle-end chart
> - opinion-and-reasons chart
> - informal outline

 Include all pieces of information required by the writing prompt. For instance, the assignment on page 174 reminds you to respond to at least one objection to your viewpoint. Refer to your T-chart or pro-con chart to find objections.

In the example outline below, the writer has used formal Roman numerals to number the paragraphs. However, she has used informal bullets to list supporting details for each paragraph. She underlined key organizational phrases. This is the method that made the most sense to her. Similarly, you should use a method that makes sense to you.

I. <u>My opinion</u>: Homework is helpful.

II. <u>Reason 1</u>: helps me practice new material
   - new types of math problem
   - long English writing assignments

III. <u>Reason 2</u>: helps me share schoolwork with my parents
   - I explain it to them
   - they help me if I have trouble
   - <u>Objection</u>: Homework takes away from family time.
   - <u>My response</u>: Be creative about what family time is.

IV. <u>Reason 3</u>: helps me plan my time
- time to do required things
- time to do fun things
- helpful habit in life

V. <u>My conclusion</u>: Helps me learn, connect with parents, manage time = necessary.

## Writing Your Test Essay

Now it's time to write your essay. This is the part of your test that will be scored, so use your best handwriting, spell out all words instead of using abbreviations, and follow your outline carefully.

For many students, the hardest part of writing an essay test is getting started. The blank page stares up at you, reminding you that each sentence you write will be carefully evaluated. Don't let this kind of thinking waste precious time. A quick and simple way to get started is to

(1) write a sentence that identifies the topic
(2) write one or several sentences explaining the topic
(3) write a sentence stating your opinion about the topic

Before you know it, your first paragraph is done!

At our school, people disagree about whether homework is necessary. I receive homework assignments for several classes every day. Usually, the homework for one class takes me around twenty minutes to do. If I have homework for three classes, for example, it takes me around an hour to do. Sometimes I spend an hour and a half. The next day at school, I turn in the work for homework credit. More important, the homework has prepared me for that day in school. Homework helps me.

(1) the topic

(2) explanation of the topic

(3) writer's opinion

Once you've got the introduction, you need to support your opinion. Your outline will tell you what to write, and in what order. Focus on getting your ideas down in clear sentences.

## Polishing Your Test Essay

In a 55-minute test period, use the final 15 minutes to revise and edit your essay. A useful guideline is to use around 10 minutes to make revisions and 5 minutes to edit.

Take a look at this paragraph from the model essay. During the writer's revision process, she marked sentences for removal, she added a transition, and she made her final point more clear.

> The most important way that homework helps me is that it makes me plan my time. I have to set aside one or one and a half hours every night for homework. ~~I make this time easier by playing soft music and having a snack and drink at the same time. I work in my room, where my little brother can't interrupt me.~~ This is not always fun. I get an hour and a half to do whatever I want. I have earned it. But after that, I know that managing my time will help me in life. because everyone has to balance work and play.

## Evaluating a Persuasive Test Essay

Teachers will evaluate your test essay using a rubric like the one they use for non-test essays. They will take into account the fact that you wrote this test in one sitting, in a limited amount of time.

# Persuasive Test Essay Rubric

| | 4<br>Strong | 3<br>Effective | 2<br>Developing | 1<br>Beginning |
|---|---|---|---|---|
| **Ideas** | The writer wrote to the prompt. Reasons are convincing. | The writer wrote to the prompt but included a few unrelated details. | The main idea relates to the prompt, but many details are unrelated. | The writer did not write to the prompt. Reasons are unconvincing or absent. |
| **organization** | Reasons are arranged from least to most important. | The most important reason is clear but not placed last. | The reasons do not have a clear sequence of least to most important. | Reasons, if present, are included in no particular order. |
| **voice** | The voice shows concern or enthusiasm balanced with trustworthiness. | Several paragraphs show concern, enthusiasm, and/or trustworthiness. | A few sentences show concern, enthusiasm, or trustworthiness. | Writing is mechanical, with no sense of a reliable writer behind the words. |
| **word choice** | Words are accurate and fair. | Most words are accurate and fair. | Many words are used incorrectly or express unfair ideas. | The incorrect use of words is confusing or misleading. |
| **sentence fluency** | A variety of sentence types is used in a pleasing rhythm. | A variety of sentence types is used, but some may be awkward. | Sentences are complete but are mostly short and simple. | Sentences are mostly of one type or are incomplete. |
| **conventions** | Few errors in capitalization, spelling, punctuation, or grammar are present. | Several errors in capitalization, spelling, punctuation, or grammar are present. | Errors in conventions do not prevent understanding. | Errors in conventions make it hard to understand the essay. |

# Evaluate a Model Test Essay

Work with a partner to evaluate the following model composition.
Use the rubric on page 180 and write your score here: _____. In a
class discussion, explain the score that you gave.

### Homework Helps Me

At our school, people disagree about whether homework is necessary. I
personally receive homework assignments for several classes every day. Usually,
the homework for one class take me around twenty minutes to do. If I have
homework for three classes, for example, it takes me around an hour to do.
Sometimes I spend an hour and a half. The next day at school, I turn in the work
for homework credit. More important, the homework have prepared me for that
day in school. Homework helps me.

One way that homework helps me is that it helps me get practice with new
material. When we learn a new kind of math problem I need to practice it on
my own. We don't have enough class time for me to get extra practice in class.
Working extra problems at home let me learn in a no-pressure setting. When
we get a writing assignment in English class, I don't have time to do all the work
in class. I like to think about things a lot. I need to do some of the work at home.
This helps me get a better grade.

Another way that homework helps me is that it gives me a way to talk about
my schoolwork with my parents. Sometimes my mom or dad sit down to look at
my homework. I show them what I was doing and ask questions. Sometimes, my
class work is new or interesting to them, and I get to be the teacher and explain
it. Other times, I need extra help. They can be my tutor. Some people say that
homework takes away from family time. You just have to be creative about what
"family time" is.

The most important way that homework helps me is that it makes me plan my
time. I have to set aside one or one and a half hours every night for homework.

I make this time easier by playing soft music and having a snack and drink at the same time. I work in my room, where my little brother can't interrupt me. This is not always fun. But after that, I get an hour and a half to do whatever I want. I have earned it. I know that managing my time will help me in life, because everyone has to balance work and play.

   Homework helps me learn connect with my parents and manage my time. For these reasons I believe that short homework assignments is a necessary part of learning at our school.

### Write a Persuasive Test Essay

Practice what you have learned by completing the following task.

**Instructions**
You have 55 minutes to complete the written composition. Read the prompt below. Then use separate paper to plan and draft your composition. Only your draft will be scored.

**Writing Prompt:**
Few people have everything they want. What is something you want but your parents won't agree to let you have? Perhaps it is a special possession, a privilege, or a special class. Think of reasons why you should have a particular thing you want. Think of what you could say to change your parents' minds. Write an essay to persuade your parents to allow you to have the possession, privilege, or class that you want.

**Remember to**
- write about the assigned topic
- state a clear thesis
- use convincing reasons and examples
- respond to at least one objection to your viewpoint
- edit your writing to correct mistakes in capitalization, spelling, punctuation, and grammar

# Persuasive Writing Wrap-Up

The activities and information in these pages will help you continue to strengthen your persuasive-writing skills. In You Be the Judge, use the Persuasive Writing Rubric to evaluate a student's work. The Ideas for Writing are additional persuasive-writing prompts you can use for practice. And finally, in the Unit 3 Reflections, you can list important ideas you have learned in this unit and set goals for future learning.

## You Be the Judge

Use what you've learned about the traits of persuasive writing to evaluate a student essay. First, review the traits of persuasive writing on page 127. Next, read the student essay printed below. Finally, in the rubric that follows the essay, assign the essay a score for each writing trait. In the space provided, explain each score that you assign.

### Stop Talking, Start Driving

by Lisa D., Cumberland, RI

Two thousand six hundred. That's the estimated number of people killed every year by automobile accidents involving cell phones. However, research is limited. The actual number could very well be 8,000. People die every day just because other drivers decide they need to send a text, make a call, or answer the phone while driving.

Cell-phone use while operating an automobile should be banned. The number of people who have died and those who die every day because of cell phones distracting drivers is outrageous. And that's just fatalities. Nonfatal injuries are a hundred times more common: approximately 330,000 per year. The number killed and injured for no good reason is much more than what it should be: zero.

These accidents could be prevented and all of these lives saved. "Chatty motorists are less adept than drunken drivers with blood alcohol levels exceeding 0.08," Robert Roy Britt wrote in *LiveScience*, citing a recent study. This means that drivers on cell phones are less skilled than people who are under the influence. According to the study, drivers using a cell phone were 12 percent slower at reacting to brake lights and took 17 percent longer to regain speed after they braked. The use of cell phones impacts the overall flow of traffic, slowing it down. As you can see, talking on a cell phone really does negatively affect your driving.

Five states—California, Connecticut, New Jersey, New York, and Washington—and the District of Columbia have banned handheld phone use by drivers, but that means 45 states haven't.

Then there's the debate about hands-free devices. Are they safe to use? The scientists who conducted the cell-phone safety study "found that even hands-free cell-phone use distracted drivers. ... Drivers look but don't see, because they're distracted by the conversation," wrote Britt in *LiveScience*. Drivers are too preoccupied with their conversations to react to everyday occurrences such as braking at stop lights, stop signs, yield signs, etc.

Another research group conducted a similar experiment in Illinois. "With younger adults, everything got worse," said Arthur Kramer, who led the study. "Both young adults and older adults tended to show deficits in performance. They made more errors in detecting important changes and they took longer to react to the changes." So even with hands-free devices, you are still at risk of causing an accident and injuring or killing yourself or others.

The most troubling question of all is, will a law make a difference? Or will drivers ignore it? A law won't eliminate the problem but perhaps it will raise awareness that cell-phone use while driving isn't smart. If more people understand the risks, maybe they will be less likely to use their phones while driving.

Every year 42,000 people die in automobile accidents. Two thousand six hundred of those are because someone was using a cell phone. Many of those deaths could have been prevented. So think twice next time you consider calling about your haircut on Tuesday while you're driving. Think again before texting a friend to say hello while you're speeding down the highway. Think about the people on the road—mothers, fathers, daughters, sons, yourself—whose lives you are risking. If we stop cell phone use while driving, many lives could be saved each year. Two thousand six hundred, to be exact.

# Persuasive Writing Rubric

|  | 4 Strong | 3 Effective | 2 Developing | 1 Beginning |
|---|---|---|---|---|
| **Ideas** Score_____ | *explanation:* | | | |
| **organization** Score_____ | *explanation:* | | | |
| **voice** Score_____ | *explanation:* | | | |
| **word choice** Score_____ | *explanation:* | | | |
| **sentence Fluency** Score_____ | *explanation:* | | | |
| **conventions** Score_____ | *explanation:* | | | |

# Ideas for Writing

The assignments that follow will give you additional practice with persuasive writing. Your teacher may choose one or let you pick one that's most interesting to you.

1. What is a hot topic at your school? Perhaps it's a big issue, such as safety or overcrowding. Perhaps it's a smaller issue, such as an unpopular rule. Choose a topic that people are buzzing about

and write a 300-word editorial for your school paper in which you

- take a position on the topic
- use a persuasive strategy to convince readers to agree with you (See the list of persuasive strategies on page 163.)

2. What is your philosophy of food? What guidelines do you follow when you choose what and how much to eat? Some people wouldn't dream of a day without chocolate, while others wouldn't dream of eating meat. What is your viewpoint on food, and how is it different from that of your friends? Write an essay of 350–400 words to persuade your friends to share your view on food. Use reasons and examples to support your ideas.

3. What activities do you enjoy outside of school? Which of these activities do you think other people your age would enjoy? Write a brochure in which you persuade readers to try a new, non-school-related activity. Develop your own topic, or choose from these options: learn a new language, read for pleasure, recycle, become a volunteer. In your brochure, be sure to use a specific persuasive strategy, clear writing, supporting images, and white space.

4. Choose an editorial or persuasive essay that you or a classmate wrote for this unit. Take the opposing viewpoint and write an editorial or essay to convince the same audience to agree with you. How does this exercise teach you more about the hot topic? Did you change your own mind while defending a different viewpoint?

# Unit 3 Reflections

How are you different as a writer now that you have completed this unit on persuasive writing? What new knowledge do you have? How is your writing stronger? What kinds of things could you work on to become even stronger as a persuasive writer? Use the following space to reflect on your work in this unit and to set goals for the future.

## Focus on Me: My Achievements as a Persuasive Writer

What I've learned about persuasive writing in this unit:

Ways my persuasive writing is stronger now:

Things I can do to practice my skills of persuasive writing:

# Literary Writing

## Get to Know the Genre: Literary Writing

**Literary writing** is a huge and delightful category. It includes all kinds of creative writing, including plays, novels, biographies, and poetry. Some literary works, such as the personal narrative, tell about real people and events. Others, such as short stories, tell about imaginary people and events. Poetry expresses ideas and emotions in the form of lines and stanzas.

When we talk about literary writing, we use special terms. Some of the terms you need to know are explained in the following mini-glossary.

## Mini-Glossary: Literary Terms

**dialogue**   The conversation between characters in a story. A character's spoken words.

**figurative language**   The use of words and phrases in a creative way instead of a literal way. The reader must use imagination to interpret figurative language. Examples of figurative language are similes and metaphors.

**narrative**   A work that tells a story about real or imaginary people and events.

**narrator**   The character or voice that tells a story. In fiction, the narrator may be a character in the story or an outside voice. In nonfiction (true stories), the narrator may be the author's voice or an outside voice.

**speaker**   The character or voice that expresses the ideas in a poem. Often, the speaker is not the same as the author.

**stanza**   A group of lines arranged together in a poem. A blank line separates stanzas.

**theme**   The main message or lesson of a literary work.

**unity**   The state in which the actions, events, ideas, and details of a work all support one theme.

> I visualize the characters completely. . . . I know how they speak, what they want, who they are, nearly everything about them.
> —JOYCE CAROL OATES (American author, 1938–)

Many people write literary works for the enjoyment it brings them. In school, you may sometimes be asked to write a story or poem. This is an opportunity to show what you know about these types of writing. This unit will guide you through the process of writing three types of literary works: a personal narrative, a short story, and a poem. Finally, you'll learn how to respond to a literary writing prompt on a test.

Literary writing includes the same six traits as the other forms of writing you have studied. The table below explains how these traits help to make literary writing strong.

## Six Traits of **Literary Writing**

| Ideas | The work is unified by one theme. |
|---|---|
| organization | Narratives have a beginning, a middle, and an end, with a clear sequence of events. Poems are arranged in lines and stanzas. |
| voice | The writer or main character shines through as a real person with an interesting attitude toward the subject of the work. |
| word choice | Words and figurative language create vivid pictures and emotions for the reader. |
| sentence fluency | Narratives use a variety of sentence types and sentence beginnings. Poems have a rhythm to the lines. |
| conventions | Quotation marks enclose spoken words. Spelling and capitalization are correct. |

Real-World Example

In the poem on the next page, the speaker is Billie Holiday. Although the speaker is fictional, she is based on the real Billie Holiday, a talented jazz singer. In this poem, she tells what it was like trying to make a name for herself.

**Ideas:** The title identifies the poem's theme: things that make the speaker happy.

## This Is Heaven to Me

Carole Boston Weatherford

**Conventions:** Each sentence in the poem begins with a capital letter, but each line of the poem does not.

**Word choice:** alliteration

**Word choice:** Vivid adjectives help the reader create a mental picture.

**Voice:** Using a vulgar expression like this shows the writer's style and emphasizes the poverty of the musicians.

Harlem sizzled after dark:
crowded theaters, jumping
dance halls, classy supper clubs,
hole-in-the-wall cafés and taverns,
musty cellars and lounges,
and a rib joint or bar and grill
on every bustling block.
I played more rundown joints
than I can recall; gigs, a blur
of smoke clouds, spotlights,
and struggling musicians like me
with barely a pot to pee in
or a window to throw it out of;
no fame or money yet;
just the thrill of fronting a band
and triggering applause.
That was enough
to put me on cloud nine.

**Sentence fluency:** The poem is made up of three sentences, ending with this short one.

## Give It a Try: Examine the Real-World Example

Can you find additional examples of the traits of good writing in the model poem above? On separate paper, list three traits of writing. For each one, quote or describe an example from the model.

# Get Ready to Write

Now that you've explored the qualities of literary writing, you're ready to create some literary pieces of your own. In the chapters that follow, you'll write a personal narrative about a choice you regretted, a short story about the supernatural, a poem about a strong emotion, and a narrative about overcoming an obstacle. You'll use the stages of the writing process—prewriting, drafting, revising, editing, and publishing—and you'll be presented with models and mini-lessons along the way.

As you work through these chapters, you can enrich your understanding by trying the suggestions below. These tips will help you connect what you're learning in this unit to your own life and the world around you.

## LEARNING TIPS

- Ask a teacher if you can create a Literary Bulletin Board, where students can hang examples of their work, share tips, suggest useful Web sites, and so on.

- Practice using literary writing to make your notes and e-mails to friends more interesting.

- Browse literary writing at a library. Find out what kinds of literary writing you like and check out one or two books to read.

- Create a poster that explains your favorite type of literary writing, with a list of recommended reading. Get permission to display it in the classroom or explain it in an oral presentation.

- Form a literary club with friends, even if it meets only once or twice this year. Share your own literary writing or read aloud from published works.

# Write a
# Personal Narrative

In this chapter, the spotlight is on *you*. As you go through the process of writing a personal narrative, you will think about yourself, talk about yourself, and write about yourself. You can be completely honest, or you can make up details, events, and conversations to fit the purpose of your story. Ultimately, your story will reveal something about yourself to your reader.

In a personal narrative, the writer shares a sequence of events that shows how he or she resolved a conflict or confronted a truth. For example, the story may be about how the writer faced his fear of singing in public. Or a story may be about how the writer turned an embarrassing moment into a moment of triumph. The purpose of writing a personal narrative is to draw in readers and make them feel as if they are right there, experiencing the events of the story.

## Six Traits of a **Personal Narrative**

| Ideas | The writer focuses on one main conflict to be resolved. Each scene and dialogue relates to this conflict. |
|---|---|
| organization | The order of events is clear. |
| voice | The writer uses the first-person point of view. The writer's personality and attitudes about the events shine through. |
| word choice | The writer balances realistic, everyday language with words that keep the reader interested. |
| sentence fluency | Sentences in dialogue show realistic speech patterns. Narrative sentences are complete. |
| conventions | Quotation marks are used correctly. Proper nouns are capitalized. Spelling and grammar are correct. |

In the story below, the writer tells how he began the first day of a new school year.

## Get Out of My Way!

It was the first day of the new school year, and I was buzzing with excitement. This would be MY year! I would have tons of friends this year. No more Mr. Anonymous.

I hurried down the sidewalk on my way to school, and I saw other kids walking to school too. Ahead of me was a kid I hadn't seen before. He was dressed in really embarrassing clothes, and he walked with a weird limp. As I watched, he tripped on a crack in the sidewalk and fell.

"Outta my way!" I said, laughing, as I zoomed past him. Later that day, I would regret that action.

As it turned out, this kid wasn't wearing "embarrassing" clothes––he was wearing a new fashion line that his mom designed and that all the girls LOVED on him. And the limp? A skateboarding injury, which only made him even more popular.

And me? I could have been Mr. Popularity's friend, but instead I'm the guy who said, "Outta my way!"

## Give It a Try: Examine the Model Story

Use the model story above to answer the following questions. Write your answers on separate paper. Then, in a class discussion, explain your answers.

1. **Ideas.**
   a. What main thing does the narrator want?
   b. How does he mess up his chances of getting what he wants?

2. **Organization.** List three different things the narrator does, in the order in which he does them.

3. **Voice and word choice.** List two words that show the narrator's personality or attitudes.

4. **Sentence fluency.** Is the narrator's spoken sentence a complete or an incomplete sentence? Why do you think this is?

5. **Conventions.** Copy the sentence that contains the narrator's spoken words, including quotation marks and punctuation marks. In a class discussion, tell why the exclamation mark is inside the quotation mark.

## Your Turn to Write: Compose a Personal Narrative

Now you'll write your own personal narrative. Read the assignment carefully and follow the strategies and instructions for each stage of the writing process.

## Assignment

Sometimes we learn truths about life the hard way. We make mistakes, we make enemies, or we let a good opportunity pass by. Think about a time when you made a choice or took an action that turned out disappointingly, or worse. What happened to make you regret what you did? Who was involved? What led you to make the choices you did? What were your thoughts when it was all over?

Write a 400-word narrative for your classmates to read, telling about an action, choice, or decision that didn't turn out well. To help your readers feel as though they are sharing your experience, be sure to

- focus on one specific action, choice, or decision
- make the order of events clear
- use words and dialogue that sound natural and interesting
- show how things ended, or were resolved

Prewrite

**Analyze the Prompt.** What does the prompt tell you about your goals for this assignment? Read the assignment closely to find answers to the following questions. Use separate paper.

1.  What is the purpose of this personal narrative?
2.  Who is the audience for this personal narrative?
3.  How long does the personal narrative need to be?

**Choose a Topic.** Which action, choice, or decision would you like to tell about in a personal narrative? List ideas for topics in each category below. Then circle the topic you think would make the best story. A few ideas are written in the table to help spark your own ideas.

**If I could go back in time and change some things, I would. For example . . .**

| Actions | Choices | Decisions |
|---|---|---|
| when I sneaked my handheld game to school, against the rules | when I chose popularity over friendship | the time I decided to quit being Mike's friend |
|  |  |  |

**Gather Ideas and Details.** In the following table, fill in details to answer each question about the action, choice, or decision that you are writing about.

### 5 Ws Plus H Table

| | |
|---|---|
| Who? | |
| What? | |
| When? | |
| Where? | |
| Why? | |
| How? | |

**Organize Ideas and Details.** Create a **timeline** to organize the events of your personal narrative. Begin with the first important action, conversation, or thought that leads to the action, choice, or decision. Then continue listing actions, conversations, or thoughts in order, leading up to the moment when you realized your mistake or felt regret. You can organize your timeline by listing things in one of these ways:

- day of the week
- time of day
- simple sequence (first, second, third, etc.)

1. I lie and tell Mom that students can take games to school today.
2. Mom tells me to leave the game at home.
3. I take the game anyway.
4. I hide the game in my sweatshirt at the bottom of my book bag.
5. Dad finds the game.
6. I get grounded.
7. My parents don't trust me anymore, which puts major limits on my social life.

## Draft

Since your personal narrative is about something that happened to you, you'll write your story using the first-person point of view. You are the central character of your story. You will tell about actions and conversations from your own point of view. What did *you* see? What did *you* hear? What did *you* think, suspect, say, or do? Use first-person pronouns such as *I, me, my, myself, we, our,* and *us*.

Here are the first few paragraphs of a story about a boy who sneaks a new game to school, against the rules. The first-person pronouns are underlined, to help you study the first-person point of view.

If I could go back in time and change things, I would. This is what happened.

My mom left early for work, as she often does. I finished getting ready for school, as I always do. The bus would be here in fifteen minutes.

I packed my new portable electronic game in my backpack. Once I was sure Mom was out of the neighborhood, I called her cell phone.

**Write Your Personal Narrative.** Using the timeline you created, write your personal narrative. Make sure that your story has a beginning, a middle, and an end.

- The **beginning** sets the stage for the story. Hook your reader's interest by creating curiosity about the action, choice, or decision that forms the focus of the story.
- The **middle** of the story leads up to and includes the action, choice, or decision. You also want to tell what happened just afterward, to show why it didn't turn out well. Keep the story moving by telling what people say and do. Brief descriptions that help your reader create a mental picture are great. However, don't give long descriptions that bring the story to a standstill.
- The **end** brings the story to a close. Tell why you wish you could redo things, how you changed as a result of the events, or some other personal response. Just as the experience was meaningful to you, you can help it be meaningful to your reader, too.

## Revise

You have a complete draft of your personal narrative. It tells who, what, when, where, why, and how about an action, choice, or decision in your past. It ends by giving your response to the key event. This is a strong start, and you should feel a sense of accomplishment.

Now, during the revision stage, focus on making each part of your story stronger. This is the time to clarify actions, statements, or thoughts. This is the time to cut out details or sentences that do not move the plot forward. The checklist on the next page will help you make some revisions.

**Revise Your Personal Narrative.** Use the following checklist to revise the rough draft of your story. The Personal Narrative Rubric that follows the checklist will help you determine how strong your story is and where to make changes.

### Ideas

❑ Underline the sentence(s) where you reveal the focus of the story (one main action, choice, or decision). Revise your narrative if it lacks a specific focus.

❑ Does each action, conversation, and thought help to move the story forward? Remove any irrelevant details.

### Organization

❑ Does the narrative have a beginning, a middle, and an end?

❑ Is the order of events clear?

### Voice

❑ Do you use the first-person point of view consistently?

❑ Write *voice* above three words or phrases that show your personality or attitudes.

### Word choice

❑ Do you use realistic words in your dialogue?

❑ Circle three interesting, vivid words you used to keep your reader's interest.

### Sentence fluency

❑ Check that you used complete sentences to tell about actions and events.

❑ Have you used realistic speech patterns in dialogue? (For instance, since people do not always speak in complete sentences, the dialogue in your story may contain realistic-sounding sentence fragments.)

# Personal Narrative Rubric

| | 4 Strong | 3 Effective | 2 Developing | 1 Beginning |
|---|---|---|---|---|
| Ideas | One conflict is resolved through relevant actions and dialogue. | One conflict is resolved. Most actions and dialogue clearly relate. | Actions and dialogue are only loosely related to the conflict. | The conflict is not clear. Actions and dialogue do not seem related. |
| organization | The story has a beginning, a middle, and an end. Order of events is clear. | The story has a beginning, a middle, and an end. Order of events is mostly clear. | The beginning or end of the story is unclear. Order of events is sometimes unclear. | The story needs structure. Events are included in no particular order. |
| voice | The writer uses first-person point of view consistently. The writer's personality and attitudes shine through. | First-person point of view is used most of the time. The writer's personality and attitudes are evident. | First-person point of view is not used consistently. The writer's personality and attitudes are hard to identify. | The writer does not use the first-person point of view. No particular personality or attitude is evident. |
| word choice | Realistic words are balanced with interesting word choices. | Realistic words are balanced with several interesting word choices. | Realistic words are balanced with one or two interesting word choices. | Word choices are basic. Interesting words are needed. |
| sentence fluency | Most sentences are complete. Sentence fragments make dialogue sound realistic. | Two or three sentence fragments are used outside of dialogue. | Sentence fragments are distracting and difficult to understand. | Many sentence fragments are used, making it hard to understand the story. |
| conventions | Quotation marks, capitalization, and verb forms are used correctly. | There are several mistakes in the use of quotation marks, capitalization, or verb forms. | There are many mistakes in the use of quotation marks, capitalization, and verb forms. | Mistakes in conventions make the story hard to understand. |

## Edit

During the editing stage of your writing process, check to make sure that you have used quotation marks correctly. **Quotation marks** indicate the beginning and end of a character's spoken words. Look closely at the quotation marks in these paragraphs from the model story.

> "Mom!" I said when she answered. "I forgot to tell you that today, students are allowed to bring games to school. I'm taking my new game."
>
> "I'm not buying it," she said. "Leave your game at home." And she hung up. Just like that.

In the example above, notice the use of punctuation marks with quotation marks. A comma or a period goes inside the closing quotation mark. A question mark or exclamation mark goes inside the closing quotation mark if it is part of the character's spoken sentence.

Besides editing your work for correct use of quotation marks, edit for the correct forms of *irregular verbs*. The following mini-lesson explains.

## Mini-Lesson: Using Irregular Verbs

As you know, every complete sentence has at least one verb. Since a verb can take different forms, it is important to use the correct forms of verbs when you write. Doing so helps your reader follow the action and dialogue without confusion.

Most verbs are *regular verbs*. This means that they form their past and past participles by adding *-d* or *-ed* to the present-tense form.

## Regular Verbs

| Present | Past | Past Participle |
| --- | --- | --- |
| help | helped | (has) helped |
| open | opened | (has) opened |
| smile | smiled | (has) smiled |
| talk | talked | (has) talked |
| wave | waved | (has) waved |

Some verbs are *irregular verbs*. They form their past and past participles by changing the spelling of the word, but not by adding -*d* or -*ed*. Different irregular verbs spell their past and past participle forms in different ways. For this reason, we must learn each one separately.

The following table shows the forms of some commonly used irregular verbs.

## Irregular Verbs

| Present | Past | Past Participle |
| --- | --- | --- |
| buy | bought | (has) bought |
| drink | drank | (has) drunk |
| eat | ate | (has) eaten |
| feel | felt | (has) felt |
| find | found | (has) found |
| get | got | (has) gotten |
| go | went | (has) gone |
| hear | heard | (has) heard |
| hold | held | (has) held |
| ride | rode | (has) ridden |
| run | ran | (has) run |
| say | said | (has) said |
| sing | sang | (has) sung |
| think | thought | (has) thought |
| wear | wore | (has) worn |

## Give It a Try: Write the Forms of Verbs

Read the following paragraphs from the model story. Ten regular and irregular verbs are underlined. Using these verbs, create a table showing the present, past, and past participle forms of each underlined verb (like the table on page 205). Complete your work on your own paper and then share your answers in a class discussion.

At the end of the school day, I <u>wrapped</u> the game carefully in an extra sweatshirt I <u>had</u> in my locker, and I <u>stuffed</u> it in the bottom of my bag. Even if Mom <u>checked</u> my bag, she wouldn't <u>find</u> the game.

Once I <u>got</u> home, I <u>tossed</u> my bag on my bed and <u>went</u> downstairs to <u>eat</u> leftover nachos from dinner last night. "Life is good," I <u>said</u> to myself with a chuckle.

## Give It a Try: Use the Correct Forms of Irregular Verbs

Edit the rough draft of your personal narrative, paying close attention to verb forms. Make sure that you have used the correct form of each irregular verb. If you are not sure of the correct form, consult a grammar handbook or a reliable grammar Web site.

## Edit

**Edit Your Personal Narrative.** Edit the revised copy of your story. The following questions will help you decide what to change, remove, or leave in place.

### Conventions
❏  Did you capitalize the names of people, schools, and other proper nouns?

❑ Did you use the first-person point of view consistently?

❑ Did you enclose a character's spoken words in quotation marks?

❑ Did you use the correct forms of irregular verbs?

❑ Did you correct spelling mistakes, either with a friend's help or by using a dictionary?

---

**T!p** — Be sure to give your story a title that will grab your reader's interest. At the same time, the title should give the reader some idea of what the story is about. Choose a title that hints at the key action, choice, or decision, or that uses an interesting phrase from the story.

---

## PUBLISH

**Presentation.** Prepare your narrative for publication by writing or typing the final, edited copy.

**Publish.** Here are ideas for publishing your personal narrative.

❑ Create a podcast of your story.

❑ Read your story aloud to the class.

❑ Read your story to your family at dinner tonight.

❑ Post a copy of your story to your personal Web page.

❑ Mail a copy of your story to a friend or family member.

## Evaluate Your Narrative

Your teacher will either assess your narrative, ask you to self-assess your narrative, or ask you to switch with a partner and assess each other's work.

## Evaluate the Model Personal Narrative

Work with a partner to evaluate the following model personal narrative. Use the rubric on page 203 and write your score here: _____. In a class discussion, explain the score that you gave.

## A Sneak and a Liar

If I could go back in time and change things, I would. This is what happened.

My mom left early for work, as she often does. I finished getting ready for school, as I always do. The bus would be here in fifteen minutes.

I packed my new portable electronic game in my backpack. Once I was sure Mom was out of the neighborhood, I called her cell phone.

"Mom!" I said when she answered. "I forgot to tell you that today, students are allowed to bring games to school. I'm taking my new game."

"I'm not buying it," she said. "Leave your game at home." And she hung up. Just like that.

I was upset, but hey, I can roll with the punches. I left my new game packed in my school bag. I would get home from school before Mom got home from work, so no big bad. Dad would be home early, but he wouldn't check my bag. Problem solved.

I had an adventurous day, to say the least. Two of my buddies brought their games to school, and we found a way to play at lunch and in study hall, unnoticed. Life was good!

At the end of the school day, I wrapped the game carefully in an extra sweatshirt I had in my locker, and I stuffed it in the bottom of my bag. Even if Mom checked my bag, she wouldn't find the game.

Once I got home, I tossed my bag on my bed and went downstairs to eat leftover nachos from dinner last night. "Life is good," I said to myself with a chuckle.

Then Dad came into the kitchen. He had That Look on his face.

Long story short: Mom had called Dad, and he looked in my bag. He was not stupid. He found my hidden game, and he knew I had taken it to school. Now my parents have taken away the game, and they have taken away so many, many of my privileges. Life is not good.

But you know what's worse? My parents no longer trust me. They look at me with suspicion, distrust, and doubt. It's going to take months before they believe anything I say. They might think I'm a liar for a long time. This could seriously interfere with my social life. No, life is not good.

# Write
a Story

People are born storytellers. In daily life, we tell our friends about funny events, a friend's weird behavior, or disappointing experiences. Telling stories about our lives helps us make sense of things and helps other people understand our experiences, feelings, and problems.

You can use your everyday storytelling abilities to build strong skills of telling stories on paper. In fact, you have already begun to do so. In Chapter 13, you wrote a personal narrative about real events and people. Now you'll build on your skills by writing a story about imaginary people and events.

## Six Traits of a **Story**

| Ideas | The writer focuses on one main conflict to be resolved. Each scene and dialogue relates to this conflict. |
|---|---|
| organization | The order of events is clear. |
| voice | The writer uses a consistent narrative point of view. The tone fits with how the writer wants the reader to feel after reading the narrative: amused, sad, triumphant, or something else. |
| word choice | The writer uses vivid words to help show action, feelings, thoughts, and so on. |
| sentence fluency | Sentences in dialogue show realistic speech patterns. Narrative sentences are complete. |
| conventions | Quotation marks are used to begin and end a character's words. Proper nouns are capitalized. The present tense or past tense is used consistently. Spelling is correct. |

In the story below, the main character, Norbot, faces a frightening situation.

## Creature from Outer Space

On the way to the park one day, Norbot ran into an alien. He slowed down and came to a stop. Where had this strange creature come from? Was it dangerous?

The creature moved closer on two sticklike objects. Norbot's internal temperature began to rise. What was happening? Was he being attacked? He moved backward quickly.

The creature stopped moving.

Norbot felt steam rising from his face. *Wonderful*, he thought. *The fear is making me overheat.*

A small hole opened in the creature's face, and a voice came out. It said, "Do you speak English? I landed my ship in that park over there, but I seem to be on the wrong planet. Do you have a galaxy map?"

Norbot's face cooled immediately. He swiveled on well-oiled wheels so that his back was to the alien. "Please open panel B," he said politely. "Maps of the galaxy are available by connecting to port A. Immediate payment is required."

Norbot blinked his face lights happily. Now he would be able to afford that new memory storage he had been wanting.

## Give It a Try: Examine the Model Story

Use the model story above to answer the following questions. Write your answers on separate paper. When you are finished, explain your answers in a class discussion.

1. **Ideas.** What problem does Norbot face?
2. **Organization.**
   a. Which paragraph introduces Norbot's problem?
   b. In which paragraph is Norbot's problem solved?
   c. Which paragraph shows Norbot's response to how things ended?
3. **Voice and word choice.** List three words or phrases that help bring Norbot to life on the page.
4. **Sentence fluency.** Does this story use mostly simple, compound, or complex sentences? How does the main sentence type influence the pace of the events?
5. **Conventions.** Why are some words printed in italic type?

## Your Turn to Write: Compose a Story

Now you'll create your own story. Read the assignment carefully and follow the strategies and instructions for each stage of the writing process.

## Assignment

Your school is hosting a literary festival with the theme Other Worlds. For the festival, write a 350- to 400-word story that includes at least one "otherworldly" element. For instance, the story could be set on another planet, or one of the characters could be a supernatural creature.

Write a story that students would enjoy hearing read aloud at the festival. In your story, be sure to
- write about a problem or conflict that the main character must solve
- include realistic dialogue
- include a beginning, a middle, and an end
- include an otherworldly setting or character(s)

## Prewrite

**Analyze the Prompt.** What does the prompt tell you about your goals for this assignment? Read the assignment closely to find answers to the following questions. Write your answers on separate paper.

1. What is the purpose of this story?
2. Who is the audience for this story?
3. How long does the story need to be?

**Choose a Topic.** With your teacher's permission, gather in a small group and share ideas about "otherwordly" characters and settings. The following sentence starters may help.

I've always liked fairy tales about . . .

I once read a Greek myth about a . . .

I've always wanted to visit the planet . . .

One day, robots will probably . . .

My favorite television show/movie has supernatural creatures, and they are . . .

Based on your group's discussion, choose one or more otherwordly characters or settings to use in your story. Write your choice(s) on your paper.

**Gather and Organize Ideas and Details.** You can use a story map to plan your story. On the next page is an example of how one writer planned a story about a character's discovery of a magical coin. After the model story map, you'll find a blank story map. Use that one to plan your story.

## Beginning

Who is the main character? Alicia, a scuba diver

What problem or conflict does he or she face? She comes up from a dive and finds the ocean shore populated with centaurs, griffins, nymphs, and more.

Who are the other characters? Rich, her dive team leader. Other divers.

| **Main Event 1** | **Main Event 2** |
|---|---|
| During a dive, Alicia takes a gold coin that Rick said not to touch. | The dive team comes back up, but the beach looks different. Are they at the wrong location? |

| **Main Event 3** | **Main Event 4** |
|---|---|
| Centaurs, a griffin, elves, and tree nymphs are in the forest and on the shore. | Dragon comes out of forest and roars and breathes fire at the dive team on the beach. |

## End

How does the main character solve the problem or conflict?

She goes down and puts the golden coin back where it belongs.

How does the main character feel about this solution?

Relieved. But she doesn't realize that one fairy is still there.

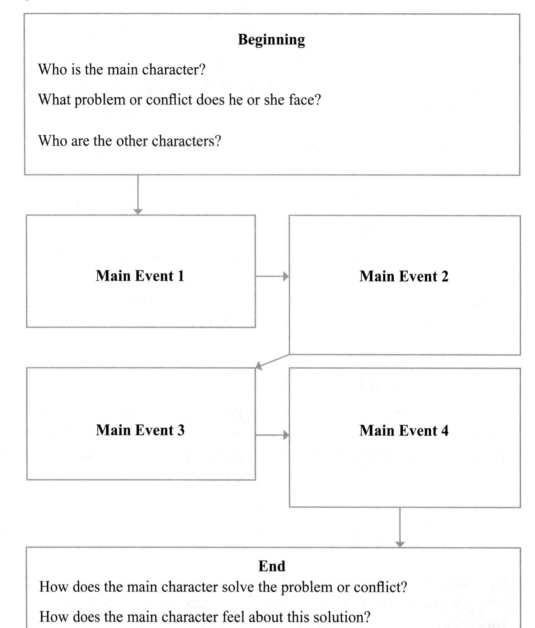

**Beginning**

Who is the main character?

What problem or conflict does he or she face?

Who are the other characters?

**Main Event 1**

**Main Event 2**

**Main Event 3**

**Main Event 4**

**End**

How does the main character solve the problem or conflict?

How does the main character feel about this solution?

# Draft

Just as you and your friends communicate by talking, the characters in stories communicate by talking. They speak to express their thoughts, to communicate with one another, and even to argue. The following mini-lesson gives helpful information about writing dialogue for your story.

## Mini-Lesson: Writing Dialogue

As you know, **dialogue** is the conversation between characters. Dialogue helps bring characters to life, it draws readers in to the characters' lives, and it helps move the story forward. Here are five tips for writing powerful dialogue.

**1. Model the dialogue on real people's speech.** Dialogue in a story should sound like people's speech in real life. To develop your ear for dialogue, spend time listening to people talk. Write down conversations that you hear, including the incomplete sentences, one-word response, and informal language.

"Over there!" Alicia said. "A griffin."

"A what?" said Rick. "That can't be real."

**2. Make every word count.** Write dialogue that is *focused* and *purposeful*. In real life, people say a lot of unnecessary things. They repeat themselves, and they go off topic. In contrast, dialogue in a story must focus the reader's attention on the conflict or problem. It should help the reader understand an action, a character, or some other part of the story.

"Hey, Rick!" she called out. "Did we surface at the wrong location?"

"Quick!" he shouted. "Back to the ocean floor!"

**3. Use speech tags.** In your story, make it clear who is saying what. The best way to do this is to use speech tags such as *said* or *asked*, along with the speaker's name.

Alicia said, "Look at that!"

Rick asked, "Is that a dragon?"

**4. Break up dialogue with actions.** Readers can easily lose interest in a conversation that goes on for too long. To keep the pace of the story moving, use a mix of dialogue and action. Play the scene in your imagination as if it were a movie. Weave together the words and actions that bring the scene to life.

"Centaurs?" Alicia said. "What's going on?"

Overhead, a large beast flew in circles. It had the body of a lion but the wings and head of an eagle.

"A griffin?" said Rick in wonder.

**5. Punctuate dialogue correctly.** Use quotation marks and other marks of punctuation correctly. Keep these three rules in mind:

- Begin and end a character's spoken words with a quotation mark.
- Place periods and ending commas inside the quotation mark.
- Place question marks and exclamation marks inside the quotation mark if they are part of the character's spoken words.

Study the examples of dialogue in this mini-lesson, noticing the placement of each mark of punctuation.

**Write Your Story.** Using your story map from page 216, write a rough draft of your story. Be sure to include actions and dialogue that move the story forward.

## Revise

Use the following checklist to revise the rough draft of your story. The Story Rubric that follows the checklist will help you determine how strong your story is and where to make revisions.

**Ideas**
❑ Does each action, conversation, and thought help to move the story forward?

**Organization**
❑ Does the narrative have a beginning, a middle, and an end?
❑ Is the order of the events and characters' thoughts clear?
❑ Have you used paragraphs to organize dialogue and chunks of action?

**Voice**
❑ Do you use the first-person or the third-person point of view? Check that you use it consistently.

**Word choice**
❑ Do you need to use a thesaurus to find a more vivid replacement for a word? Circle and revise any weak words.

**Sentence fluency**
❑ Have you used complete sentences to tell about actions and events?
❑ Have you used realistic speech patterns in dialogue?

# Story Rubric

| | 4<br>Strong | 3<br>Effective | 2<br>Developing | 1<br>Beginning |
|---|---|---|---|---|
| **Ideas** | The work is unified by one main conflict or problem to be solved. | The conflict or problem is clear, but some details do not relate. | The writer is beginning to make the conflict or problem clear. | The problem or conflict is not clear. Most details seem unrelated. |
| **Organization** | The order of actions/thoughts is clear. | Most details follow a logical order. | Organization of details is awkward. | Actions or thoughts are in random order. |
| **Voice** | The narrative point of view is consistent throughout the story. | The narrative point of view is mostly consistent. | The narrative point of view changes several times. | The narrative point of view changes often. |
| **Word Choice** | Vivid words are used throughout the story. | Most paragraphs use vivid words. | One or two paragraphs use vivid words. | Words are plain and basic. |
| **Sentence Fluency** | Sentences are varied. Dialogue is realistic. | Most paragraphs have varied sentences. Dialogue is mostly realistic. | The writer has made a few attempts to vary sentences and write realistic dialogue. | All sentences are of one length. Dialogue doesn't seem realistic. |
| **Conventions** | Quotation marks enclose spoken words. Spelling and capitalization are correct. | There are a couple of mistakes in punctuation, spelling, or capitalization. | There are many mistakes in punctuation, spelling, and capitalization. | Mistakes in conventions make the story hard to understand. |

## Edit

Edit the revised copy of your story, using the following checklist.

### Conventions
❏ Did you enclose characters' spoken words in quotation marks?
❏ Did you correct punctuation mistakes, either with a friend's help or by using a handbook?
❏ Did you correct spelling mistakes, either with a friend's help or by using a dictionary?
❏ Did you correct grammar mistakes, either with a friend's help or by using a grammar handbook?

## PUBLISH

**Presentation.** Prepare your story for publication by writing or typing the final, edited copy.

**Publish.** Here are ideas for publishing your story.
❏ Submit your story to a magazine or Web site that publishes the writing of young people.
❏ Post a copy of your story to your personal Web page.
❏ Create a podcast of your story.
❏ Work with classmates to create a self-published collection of stories. Add artwork to the collection.
❏ Host a literary festival at your home and invite friends to read their stories aloud at the festival.
❏ Read your story to an elderly person who would enjoy a visit from you.

## Evaluate Your Story

Your teacher will either assess your story, ask you to self-assess your story, or ask you to switch with a partner and assess each other's work.

## Evaluate the Model Story

Work with a partner to evaluate the following model story. Use the rubric on page 220 and write your score here: _____. In a class discussion, explain the score that you gave.

### Don't Touch!

Off the shore of Hawaii, a dive team explored the ocean's floor. Rick, the team leader, had instructed them, "Look but don't touch." Alicia was finding it hard to follow the order because all over the ocean floor were gold coins. The disks of metal twinkled in the glow of their helmet-mounted lights. Alicia couldn't help but touch a coin. Nothing happened. Swiftly, she tucked the coin into a pocket on her dive suit.

An hour later the team surfaced. As Alicia pulled the scuba mask from her face, she looked around uneasily. The shore didn't look the same.

"Hey, Rick!" she called out. "Did we surface at the wrong location?"

Rick and the other divers stared around them. Rick silently pointed toward the shore. There, at the edge of the jungle, a herd of horses stood. But they weren't exactly horses. Although they had an animal's body, they had the shoulders and heads of humans.

"Centaurs?" Alicia said. "What's going on?"

Overhead, a large beast flew in circles, looking down at them. It had the body of a lion but the wings and head of an eagle. It let out a sharp cry.

"A griffin?" said Rick in wonder.

And then they spotted more creatures. Tiny elves peered from beneath broad jungle leaves. Tree nymphs blinked large, lovely eyes; their bodies were mostly camouflaged against the trunks of trees.

Then a mighty roar shook the ground, and a blast of fire shot out of the forest. The creatures on shore instantly scattered into the forest. The roar sounded again, and a massive brown and green dragon leaped into view. He spewed out another wave of fire.

Suddenly, Alicia remembered the gold coin she had in her pocket. "Quick!" she shouted. "Back to the ocean floor!" The other divers obeyed instantly.

On the ocean floor, Alicia pulled the coin from her pocket and held it up for the others to see. Then she dropped it, letting it dance down into the water until it rested among the other coins.

When the team surfaced this time, Alicia studied the shore carefully. It looked normal again. No mythical creatures were in sight. She breathed a sigh of relief. But she didn't realize that in the trees a fairy giggled, happy to have found its way into this strange new world.

# Write a Poem

Poetry is all around us, not just in our literature textbooks. Listen, and you'll hear it in the catchy jingles in commercials and in the songs on the radio. Look closely, and you may see it in a friend's scribbled note—if you just add some line breaks and stanza breaks!

Poems have the power to tap into our emotions quickly and surprisingly. Because poems can be so powerful, many people assume that they cannot write poetry. They think it takes a special talent or a lot of training. The truth is, anybody can write a poem if he or she has something to express. Putting thoughts and feelings into lines and stanzas is easier than you might think. This chapter will show you how. You'll read a model poem, and you'll write your own poem about a theme of your choice.

## Six Traits of a **Poem**

| Ideas | The poem is unified by one theme. |
|---|---|
| organization | The words or sentences are arranged in lines and stanzas. |
| voice | The writer or speaker shines through as a real person with an interesting attitude toward the theme. |
| word choice | Words and figurative language create vivid pictures and emotions for the reader. |
| sentence fluency | Lines and stanzas of the poem have a rhythm that draws in the reader. |
| conventions | The writer's use of capitalization, punctuation, and spelling is consistent. |

In the poem below, the writer expresses ideas and emotions about a central theme.

### Love Is Like

Bubble gum whispers in my ear:
Secrets for only me to hear.
Cotton candy dreams for me.
I love you and you love me.

Holding hands in hot, hot sun,
Amusement park days of fun.
Trading promises, staying true.
You love me and I love you.

## Give It a Try: Examine the Model Poem

Use the model poem above to answer the following questions. Write your answers on separate paper. Then discuss your responses with your classmates.

1. **Ideas.** What word or phrase would you choose to express the theme of the poem?
2. **Organization.**
   a. How many stanzas does this poem have?

   b. How many lines does this poem have?

3. **Voice.** Based on the poem, what can you tell about the speaker's personality? Complete this sentence:

   The speaker in this poem is the kind of person who . . .

4. **Sentence fluency and word choice.** What is the rhyme scheme, or pattern, in this poem?
5. **Conventions.** List two rules of capitalization that the writer follows.

Your Turn to Write: Create a Poem

Now you'll compose your own poem. Read the assignment carefully and follow the strategies and instructions for each stage of the writing process.

# Assignment

A teacher at your school is creating a poetry page on the school's official Web site. Students are invited to submit poems of around 15 lines long that express ideas or emotions on a particular theme. Here are some suggested topics:

emotions such as love, loss, anger, and joy

friendship

nature

sports

family

For the poetry page, write a poem of around 15 lines that
- expresses ideas or emotions about a theme of your choice
- uses at least three different poetic techniques, such as rhyme, alliteration, simile, and personification

 ## Prewrite

**Analyze the Prompt.** What does the prompt tell you about your goals for this assignment? Read the assignment closely to find answers to the following questions. Write your answers on separate paper.
1. What is the purpose of this poem?
2. Who is the audience for this poem?
3. How long does the poem need to be?

**Choose a Topic and Gather Ideas.** What theme will you choose for your poem? Explore different themes while completing the following table about figures of speech. By the time you've completed the table, you'll have at least one great idea for a poem.

## Similes

A simile makes a comparison by using the word *like*, *as*, or *than*.

My tears fell **like** rain.
The trees were majestic **as** kings.
His mood was darker **than** night.

| Write two similes of your own, using one or more themes listed in the assignment. | 3. List ideas for poems that could use one or more of these similes. Example: *a poem about loyalty in a family* |
|---|---|
| 1. | |
| 2. | |

## Metaphors

A metaphor makes a comparison indirectly by saying that one thing *is* the other thing.

The baseball **was** a streak of white light.
The trees **were** majestic kings

| Write two metaphors of your own, using themes listed in the assignment. | 6. List ideas for poems that could use one or more of these metaphors. Example: *a poem about winning a baseball game* |
|---|---|
| 4. | |
| 5. | |

## Personification

Personification is a figure of speech in which nonhuman things are given human qualities.

A gentle **breeze whispered** secrets in my ear.
A golden **moon smiled** down at the romantic couple.
The **scoreboard mocked** us with its numbers

| Write two sentences that use personification.<br><br>7.<br><br><br><br>8. | 9. List ideas for poems that could use personification. Example: *a poem about winning a baseball game* |
|---|---|

**Organize Ideas and Details.** You can organize ideas and emotions about your theme by writing a paragraph. Doing this allows you to get ideas down on paper without worrying about the form of the poem yet. Here is an example of one writer's paragraph about feeling insecure on the first day at a new school. She builds her paragraph around the idea of the school as a monster.

The new school towers over me like a brick monster. Its windows are eyes that stare at me as if I were its next meal. Maybe I am. Slowly I drag myself up the long cement walk that cuts across packed dirt and patchy grass. Around me, kids are like bees, zooming here and there but never noticing me. Now I am at the steep front steps. They reach out like a tongue to bring me into the monster's mouth. I take a deep breath and plant one foot on the first step. I might as well conquer this monster and win the kingdom.

**Write a Paragraph.** Now you try it. Write a paragraph of approximately 75–100 words to express ideas or emotions about one of the themes listed in the assignment. Be sure to use a few examples of figurative language.

## Draft

At this point, you have chosen a theme for your poem, and you have gathered ideas to express in the poem by writing a paragraph. Now you're ready to arrange your words and sentences in lines and stanzas.

You can start by taking the sentences from your paragraph and writing them as a list, like this:

The new school towers over me like a brick monster.

Its windows are eyes that stare at me as if I were its next meal.

Maybe I am.

Slowly I drag myself up the long cement walk that cuts across packed dirt and patchy grass.

Around me, kids are like bees, zooming here and there but never noticing me.

Now I am at the steep front steps.

They reach out like a tongue to bring me into the monster's mouth.

I take a deep breath and plant one foot on the first step.

I might as well conquer this monster and win the kingdom.

As you can see, this work is beginning to look and sound more like a poem already. By placing thoughts into separate lines, you focus the reader's attention on each thought, one by one.

**Arrange Your Ideas in Lines and Stanzas.** Now it's your turn. Arrange the sentences in your paragraph in a list like the one above.

## Revise

To revise your poem, you'll need to strip away unnecessary words, leaving the bare bones of your ideas. You may need to shift some words onto different lines or change line breaks. You may want to add words or group lines into stanzas.

Here is the revised version of the model poem. Compare it to the longer, sentence-style version, above. The writer has removed some words, and she has expressed some ideas in a different, less wordy way. By cutting the words down to only the most necessary ones, the writer has packed a lot of meaning into each line of the poem.

The new school towers like a brick monster,

Eyes staring at me, its next meal.

I drag myself up the long cement walk

Between packed dirt and patchy grass.

Kids are like bees around me, busy and oblivious.

Steep steps face me now,

Reaching out like a tongue.

A deep breath. One step at a time.

I will conquer this monster and win the kingdom.

**Revise Your Poem.** Make your poem stronger by cutting out unnecessary words, adding new or vivid word choices, and making line breaks and stanzas, as you choose. The work you are doing now will add power to your poem.

Packing a lot of meaning into each line of your poem is one way to make it strong and memorable. Using figurative language, such as a simile or personification, is another way. A third way to add power to your poem is to use sound devices. The following mini-lesson explains.

## Mini-Lesson: Sound Devices in Poetry

Poets often use *sound devices* to give poems a musical quality, to create a particular tone, or to help create an emotional response in the reader. Commonly used sound devices include rhyme, alliteration, and onomatopoeia.

→ **Rhyme** is the use of the same sound at the ends of words, especially words that end lines in a poem.

*Holding hands in hot, hot **sun**,*
*Amusement park days of **fun**.*
*Trading promises, staying **true**.*
*You love me and I love **you**.*

In the stanza above, taken from the model poem on page 226, the writer uses rhyming words to create *couplets*—pairs of rhyming lines. Rhyme helps to create a musical rhythm in a poem.

# Give It a Try: Write Lines of Poetry That Rhyme

On separate paper, write a couplet (two lines that end in rhyming words). You can be funny, serious, romantic, or spooky; it's up to you.

→ **Alliteration** is the repetition of consonant sounds at the beginnings of words.

*Kids are like bees, busy and oblivious.*
(repetition of the b sound)

*Steep steps stand in my way,*
(repetition of the st sound)

*Holding hands in hot, hot sun,*
(repetition of the h sound)

Alliteration works best in words that are next to or very close to each other, as in the examples above. The effect is more subtle (less noticeable) if several words come between the words that repeat the sound.

# Give It a Try: Use Alliteration

On separate paper, write two lines of poetry. The lines can work together to express one thought, or each line can stand on its own. In each line, use two or more words to create alliteration.

→ **Onomatopoeia** is the use of words to represent the sounds they describe.

As you may know, many animal and nature sounds can be expressed with onomatopoeia, from the *quack* of a duck to the *plop* of a raindrop. Sounds that tools make (*bang*), explosive sounds (*pop*), annoying sounds (*squeak*), and much more can be expressed with a word that sounds like the sound it names.

## Give It a Try: Use Onomatopoeia

On separate paper, write two lines of poetry, and use one (or more) examples of onomatopoeia in each line.

**Use Sound Devices in Poetry.** Read the draft of your poem carefully, noticing the words and ideas. Look for opportunities to add sound devices by adding or replacing words. Include at least one sound device in your poem.

**Revise Your Poem Again.** Revise your poem again, this time using the checklist below. In addition, the Poem Rubric that follows the checklist will help you judge the strength of your poem.

### Ideas
- ❑ Check that your poem is unified by one theme.
- ❑ Does the poem have a title that hints at the theme? Add a title or revise yours if necessary.

### Organization
- ❑ Are the words and sentences arranged in lines and stanzas? Reorganize if necessary.

### Voice
- ❑ Is the speaker's voice interesting and expressive?

### Word choice
- ❑ Circle three vivid, expressive words.
- ❑ Underline two examples of figurative language.
- ❑ Underline one example of a sound technique.

### Sentence fluency
- ❑ Do the lines and stanzas flow with a pleasing rhythm, or should you change some of the line breaks or stanza breaks?

# Poem Rubric

| | 4<br>Strong | 3<br>Effective | 2<br>Developing | 1<br>Beginning |
|---|---|---|---|---|
| **Ideas** | The poem is unified by one theme. | The theme is clear, but some details do not relate. | The writer is beginning to make the theme clear. | The theme is not clear. Most details seem unrelated. |
| **organization** | The words are effectively arranged in lines and stanzas. | The words are arranged in lines and stanzas; some line breaks are awkward. | The words are arranged in lines and stanzas, but the effect is awkward. | The words are arranged in a paragraph. |
| **voice** | The speaker's ideas or emotions are clear and interesting. | The speaker's ideas or emotions are clear but don't consistently draw in the reader. | The ideas or emotions are weak; they don't consistently draw in the reader. | No clear ideas or emotions are expressed, making it hard to connect to the poem. |
| **word choice** | Figurative language and sound devices make the poem memorable. | Figurative language and sound devices make a few lines memorable. | The writer has used one example of figurative language or a sound device. | The writer has not used figurative language or a sound device. |
| **sentence fluency** | Lines and stanzas have a rhythm that draws in the reader. | Lines and stanzas have a rhythm, but a few breaks are awkward. | Lines and stanzas have many awkward breaks. | Lines and stanzas have no clear pattern or rhythm to the breaks. |
| **conventions** | Capitalization is consistent. Punctuation and spelling are correct. | There are a few mistakes in capitalization, punctuation, or spelling. | There are many mistakes in capitalization, punctuation, and spelling. | Mistakes in conventions make the poem hard to understand. |

## Edit

Edit the revised copy of your poem. Use reference tools, such as a dictionary, to help yourself identify and correct mistakes in spelling, capitalization, punctuation, and grammar.

### PUBLISH

**Presentation.** Prepare your poem for publication by writing or typing the final, edited copy.

**Publish Your Poem.** Here are ideas for publishing the final copy of your poem.
- ❑ Ask a friend to film you while you read your poem. Send a copy of the recording to a distant family member or post it to a safe Web site.
- ❑ Create a Web site where you and your friends can post your poetry for a public audience. (Check with a teacher or parent first, and follow his or her safety guidelines for dealing with public audiences.)
- ❑ With friends, create a chapbook of poetry. Enhance the themes of the poems by adding drawings and photographs to the booklet. Finally, make copies for each person who is published in the booklet. Make additional copies to give as gifts.
- ❑ Plan a stand-up poetry night where you and others can stand before a friendly audience and read your poems aloud.

## Evaluate Your Poem

Your teacher will either assess your poem, ask you to self-assess your poem, or ask you to switch with a partner and assess each other's work.

# Evaluate the Model Poem

Work with a partner to evaluate the following model poem. Use the rubric on page 235 and write your score here: _____. In a class discussion, explain the score that you gave.

Beauty and the Beast

The new school lurks like a brick monster,
Eyes staring mercilessly at me, its next meal.
I drag myself up the cracked cement walk
Between packed dirt and patchy grass.
Kids buzz like bees, busy and oblivious.
Steep steps stand in my way,
Reaching out like a tongue.
A deep breath: Whoooo. One step at a time,
I will conquer this monster and win the kingdom.

# Chapter 16

# Test Writing: The Narrative

Some people write stories in their free time, just for fun. Lots of people read stories just for fun. But why, you may wonder, would a teacher ask you to write a story on a test?

As with other forms of writing, the narrative can be a showcase for your skills of using the traits of writing. In addition, you can write a narrative to show your understanding of, or your point of view on, a particular theme. For instance, after reading a story about characters who hide a runaway slave in the 1850s, you may be asked to write a story that shows why standing up for your beliefs is worthwhile. In this way, you share your knowledge and opinions through fiction instead of nonfiction.

The following table explains how the traits of writing relate to writing a narrative on a test.

## Six Traits of a Narrative Test Essay

| | |
|---|---|
| Ideas | The writer focuses on one main conflict to be resolved. Each scene and dialogue relates to this conflict. |
| organization | The order of events is clear. |
| voice | The writer uses a consistent narrative point of view. The tone fits with how the writer wants the reader to feel after reading the narrative. |
| word choice | The writer uses vivid words to help show action, feelings, thoughts, and so on. |
| sentence fluency | Sentences in dialogue show realistic speech patterns. Narrative sentences are complete. |
| conventions | Quotation marks are used correctly to enclose a character's words. Capitalization, spelling, punctuation, and grammar are correct. |

# Preparing to Write Your Test Essay

A narrative test prompt may be linked to a passage that you read. For example, you may read a story about a drummer boy's experience during the American Civil War. Then the prompt may ask you to write a story about a modern-day character who shows patriotism.

Another type of narrative prompt stands alone instead of referring to a passage, like the one in the box below.

---

**Instructions**

You have 45 minutes to complete the written composition. Read the prompt below. Then use separate paper to plan and draft your composition. Only your draft will be scored.

**Writing Prompt**

People play team sports for many different reasons. Some people play for the love of the sport, while others don't have fun unless they win. Some people enjoy competing as part of a team, while others aren't happy unless they can lead the team. Write a story that shows what's really important in playing team sports. You can write about real or imaginary characters. Be sure your story has a beginning, a middle, and an end.

---

## 1. Study the Prompt

Take a few moments to study the prompt before you begin to write your response. Answer these important questions:

**What is the purpose of the writing assignment?** Scan the prompt for key words that tell you what kind of response to write.

**Words That Signal a Narrative Response**

| | |
|---|---|
| narrative | story |
| characters | imaginary |

**What should you write about?** Study the prompt to determine exactly what you must write. As with other types of writing prompts, look for an *imperative sentence.* In the prompt on page 240, the imperative sentence is this one:

*Write a story that shows what's really important in playing team sports.*

This sentence is your assignment in a nutshell. Look to see if other sentences give you additional information about what to write. The imperative sentence above is followed by these sentences that give important information:

*You can write about real or imaginary characters. Be sure your story has a beginning, a middle, and an end.*

**How much time do you have to write?** The sample prompt above states that the student has 45 minutes to write the narrative. If a prompt does not state a time limit, your teacher will tell you how long the testing period lasts.

## 2. Plan Your Time
After studying the prompt, make a quick plan for how to use your time. If you have 45 minutes to write the story, you could use your time as follows:

| | |
|---|---|
| 10 minutes: | Study the prompt and do prewriting. |
| 25 minutes: | Write the story. |
| 10 minutes: | Revise and edit the story. |

## 3. Prewrite
On a narrative test, you may be tempted to start writing the story and just make it up as you go along. However, the prewriting stage is too important to skip. By planning exactly what events to include in your story, and in what order, you give yourself many advantages. First, you save time by setting limits on what the story will include. Second, you are able to create a story with a clear beginning, middle, and end. Third, you don't waste time writing scenes

that don't move the story along. And fourth, you are able to budget time to revise and edit the story.

**Choose a topic.** The writing prompt tells you to write a story that shows what's really important in playing team sports—but the prompt doesn't specify which sport. Therefore, your first task is to choose a sport that you feel comfortable writing about. Here is a three-step approach to choosing a topic:

1. Jot down a list of three to five team sports that you know about.

2. Ask yourself, "Which team sport would best help me show what's really important in playing sports?"

3. Circle the sport that best answers the question in step 2. You'll write about this sport.

---

**T!p**   Within the limits of the assignment, choose a topic that you care about. Your concern and enthusiasm for the topic will shine through. For instance, in choosing a team sport, don't assume that it has to be football or basketball. It could be relay racing, Little League, gymnastics, wheelchair basketball, or something else you know about.

---

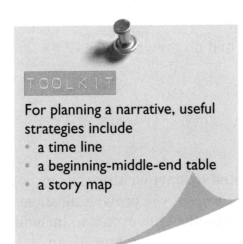

**TOOLKIT**

For planning a narrative, useful strategies include
- a time line
- a beginning-middle-end table
- a story map

**Gather ideas and details.** Next, select a strategy for choosing and organizing the characters and events of your story.

In the following model, the writer uses a beginning-middle-end table to plan a story about a character who plays Ultimate Frisbee.

---

## Beginning

<u>Characters</u>: Ryan (Red captain), Sheridan (Blue captain), Amber, other players

<u>Problem</u>: Ryan doesn't want Amber to play on his Ultimate Frisbee team because she is a girl, and he thinks girls can't compete with boys.

---

## Middle

<u>Main Event 1</u>: Ryan and other players are dividing up for a game of Ultimate Frisbee, and they need one more player. Amber asks to play.

<u>Main Event 2</u>: Ryan argues that Amber should not be allowed to play, but other players want to include her. She joins Ryan's team.

<u>Main Event 3</u>: The game starts, and Ryan tries to keep the Frisbee away from Amber. He is causing his team to lose.

<u>Main Event 4</u>: Amber catches the Frisbee and leads the team to victory.

---

## End

<u>How Ryan solves his problem</u>: He realizes that team sports is about teamwork, no matter who is on the team. When the teams divide up for a second game, Amber is his first-choice player.

---

## Writing Your Narrative Test Essay

Once you have planned what to include in our story, begin to write it. Keep yourself on track by referring to your timeline, table, or story map. Your main goal is to get the story down on paper. However, since you won't have time to recopy the story neatly, use your best handwriting now. Leave margins where you can write revisions and corrections.

Here are the opening paragraphs of the story about Ryan and Amber. Notice that the writer

- has followed his story map closely
- sets up the theme and conflict of the story right away
- uses dialogue to help move the story along

### The Ultimate Teammate

Ryan was captain of the Red team, the strongest Ultimate Frisbee team in the world! He and Sheridan, the Blue team captain, were choosing players for their teams. The problem was, they were one player short.

"Hi, guys!" said a soft voice. "Can I play? I'm pretty good at Frisbee."

Ryan frowned. "Sorry, no girls allowed," he said. To himself, he thought, *Yikes, she'd be a dead weight to her team.*

## Polishing Your Narrative Test Essay

Use the final minutes of the test period to correct mistakes in capitalization, spelling, punctuation, and grammar. You might be tempted to skip this part of the writing process, especially when time is limited. However, fixing mistakes in conventions is like removing static from a radio broadcast. As a result, your audience will be able to focus on your story, not on the "static."

Here is how the writer made corrections to one of the paragraphs in his story about Ryan and Amber. He corrected two verb forms, a sentence fragment, and a spelling mistake.

And just like that, the game *began* beginned. Ryan was sweating with anger. Hadn't he *said* no girls were allowed? Why didn't Sheridan *listen* lissen to him? Ryan was so angry. That he kept knocking over his teammates as he *tried* try to intercept the Frisbee. He didn't want Amber to even touch the Frisbee.

## Evaluating a Narrative Test Essay

When teachers evaluate a narrative test, they will be looking to see if you

- wrote to the prompt
- included only relevant details in an organized manner
- followed conventions of capitalization, spelling, punctuation, and grammar

The following rubric shows guidelines for evaluating a narrative written for a test.

# Narrative Test Essay Rubric

| | 4<br>Strong | 3<br>Effective | 2<br>Developing | 1<br>Beginning |
|---|---|---|---|---|
| **Ideas** | The work is unified by one main conflict or problem to be solved. | The conflict or problem is clear, but some details do not relate. | The writer is beginning to make the conflict or problem clear. | The problem or conflict is not clear. Most details seem unrelated. |
| **organization** | The order of actions/thoughts is clear. | Most details follow a logical order. | Organization of details is awkward. | Actions or thoughts are in random order. |
| **voice** | The narrative point of view is consistent throughout the story. | The narrative point of view is mostly consistent. | The narrative point of view changes several times. | The narrative point of view changes often. |
| **word choice** | Many vivid words are used. | A few vivid words are used. | One or two vivid words are used. | Words are plain and basic. |
| **sentence fluency** | Sentences are varied. Dialogue is realistic. | Most paragraphs have varied sentences. Dialogue is mostly realistic. | The writer has made a few attempts to vary sentences and write realistic dialogue. | All sentences are of one length. Dialogue doesn't seem realistic. |
| **conventions** | Quotation marks enclose spoken words. Spelling and capitalization are correct. | There are a couple of mistakes in punctuation, spelling, or capitalization. | There are many mistakes in punctuation, spelling, and capitalization. | Mistakes in conventions make the writing hard to understand. |

# Evaluate a Model Narrative Test Essay

Work with a partner to evaluate the following model narrative. Use the rubric on page 246 and write your score here: _____. In a class discussion, explain the score that you gave.

### The Ultimate Teammate

Ryan was captain of the Red team, the strongest Ultimate Frisbee team in the world! He and Sheridan, the Blue team captain, were choosing players for their teams. The problem was, they were one player short.

"Hi, guys!" said a soft voice. "Can I play? I'm pretty good at Frisbee."

Ryan frowned. "Sorry, no girls allowed," he said. To himself, he thought, *Yikes, she'd be a dead weight to her team.*

To Ryans surprise, Sheridan said, "Sure you can play! Everyone's welcome. My team is full, but Ryan's team has one spot left. You are on the Red team. All right everybody, let's play"

And just like that, the game beginned. Ryan was sweating with anger. Hadn't he *said* no girls were allowed? Why didn't Sheridan lissen to him? Ryan was so angry. That he kept knocking over his teammates as he try to intercept the Frisbee. He didn't want Amber to even touch the Frisbee.

"Hey, watch it!" said another frustrated Red player. "You don't own the field. We're all in this together."

Ryan stopped to glare at his teammate, just then, the Frisbee sailed over his head and Amber catched it. He watched in horror as she threw it. Then his mouth dropped open, it was actually a strong throw. Another Red player caught the Frisbee and threw it down the feild. By this time, Amber had run toward the end zone. Someone threw the Frisbee, Amber caught it, then she threw it in to score. Wow!

After that, Ryan tried his best to play hard, but mostly he just stared at Amber as she made one winning play after another. She led the team to victory.

"Great game, Red team!" said Sheridan. "How about a rematch? Maybe I'll be on the winning team this time. Ryan, who do you want to choose first for a new Red team"?

Ryan stood lost in thought. He had thought that the real reason for playing sports was to be the star himself, and to boss his team around. But Amber had prove that team sports were more fun if everyone played as a team, no matter who they was.

"I choose Amber as my first teammate! he said loudly, smiling happily."

## Write a Narrative Test Essay

Are you ready to write your own narrative in a testlike situation? Practice what you have learned by completing the following assignment.

**Instructions**
You have 45 minutes to complete the written composition. Read the prompt below. then use separate paper to plan and draft your composition. Only your draft will be scored.

**Writing Prompt**
Being a teenager can feel like flying a spaceship through an asteroid belt—you spend all your time trying not to crash into obstacles. Obstacles may include gossip, bullies, arguments, time management, and embarrassing moments. What's the secret to avoiding them? Write a story about a time when you (or an imaginary character) handled a difficult situation well. Be sure that your story has a beginning, a middle, and an end. Use dialogue to help bring your characters to life.

# Literary Writing Wrap-Up

The activities and information in these pages will help you continue to strengthen your literary-writing skills. In You Be the Judge, use the Literary Writing Rubric to evaluate a student's work. The Ideas for Writing are additional literary writing prompts you can use for practice. And finally, in the Unit 4 Reflections, you can list important ideas you have learned in this unit and set goals for future learning.

## You Be the Judge

Use what you've learned about the traits of literary writing to evaluate a student's work. First, review the traits of literary writing on page 191. Next, read the student's work printed below. Finally, in the rubric that follows, assign the work a score for each writing trait. In the space provided, explain each score that you assign.

### Warped Reality

by Sydney V., Andover, KS

Yawwwnnnn, sigh that was such a satisfying....hey wait a minuet, why am I on the floor of my parent's bedroom. Wow didn't know I could sleepwalk. Hold up, didn't I shave last night?!?! A wild thought flashed like a bullet through my mind. Sydney be rational it's six in the morning your bound to become delirious some days. Just walk to the mirror and.... AHHHHHHHHHHHHHHHH!!!!! I could not fathom the creature staring feral eyed back at me. Remarkably, the small pink nose my face once bore had elongated and was now slimy and black, ewwww and it was hairy. Oh my goodness! My hair, my once prided hair now covered my entire body! I will not let my self consider the fact that overnight I had turned into my fluffy, self-conceded Chow mix, Ginger.

"GIIINNNGGGERRRR, time for breakfast!" I abruptly realized that the individual my mother was screaming for was in my twisted reality, actually me. Dazed, as if in a dream, I stumbled into our now dull gray kitchen. I gaped down at the vile bits of lamb's dog food that was to constitute breakfast, oh yeah and also lunch and dinner. I cautiously took a nibble and immediately regretted my decision. No wonder our poor deprived dogs plead for scraps; this "food" tastes horrifying! So much for breakfast, guess I'll just attempt to ready myself for school. Hold the phone, I don't have any school!!!!!! YAY, no drawn-out boring lectures; no homework! This whole dog bit just became easier to swallow.

Sometime later my mom permitted the three of us, Rex, Maddy, and me, to explore the astounding backyard jungle. The whole day spent just lazing out in the sweet summer sun was amazing. Between slumbering underneath the shade of the lovely scented oak and wrestling with the incredibly strong and sleek beagle mix Rex, the time flew by. I hardly noticed as the others flew off the handle, barking as a Volvo pulled steadily into the driveway. MOM'S HOME!!!!!! I raced like a stallion to join my pack in waiting impatiently for the pleasant voice of my mother cooing to us as she strode toward the door, coming to play a now extremely necessary and infinitively important game of fetch.

My heart was still racing as I flopped on the ground, the moistened ball rolled out of my mouth and bounced merrily along the hardwood flooring in the dinning room. I was pooped! My long day as my dog was exceedingly amusing, but I was antsy to be myself again and eat some acceptable food. I managed to guardedly devour half of the unacceptable morsels that lay staring blankly at me from the bowl. Exhausted and in need of major beauty rest to divest myself of all this hair, I stalked to my parents spacious master bedroom and collapsed on the glorious-feeling cloud. I allowed sleep to slowly envelope my tired body.

I awoke slowly to find my mother ogling down at me, "Sydney, why in the world are you sleeping in Ginger's bed, good lord child have you completely lost your mind!" I managed a sheepish smile, "You will never believe me if I told you." I said through a giggle. My mother continued to stare at me all day, especially when I begged her with pleading eyes to play fetch with me.

# Literary Writing Rubric

| | 4 Strong | 3 Effective | 2 Developing | 1 Beginning |
|---|---|---|---|---|
| **Ideas** Score_____ | *explanation:* | | | |
| **organization** Score_____ | *explanation:* | | | |
| **voice** Score_____ | *explanation:* | | | |
| **word choice** Score_____ | *explanation:* | | | |
| **sentence fluency** Score_____ | *explanation:* | | | |
| **conventions** Score_____ | *explanation:* | | | |

# Ideas for Writing

The assignments on this page will give you additional practice with literary writing. Your teacher may choose one or let you pick one that's most interesting to you.

1. Nobody's perfect, but nobody is completely *imperfect* either! We all have moments when we do the right thing, achieve a goal, make a positive difference in someone's life, or show maturity in a difficult situation. Write a story of 350–400 words for your family to read. Tell about something you did that makes you proud of yourself.

2. Every story has at least two sides to it. For example, "The Ultimate Teammate" in Chapter 16 could be retold from Amber's point of view. Events, thoughts, and dialogue would show Amber's side of the story instead of Ryan's. Choose a story that you wrote for this unit and rewrite it from a different character's point of view. Change and add events and dialogue, as necessary, to show how this character dealt with the conflict.

3. *Narrative poems*, like "The Raven" or "Paul Revere's Ride," tell a story of an important event in the main character's life. Narrative poems often contain dialogue, and they may or may not use rhyme. Like other poems, a narrative poem is arranged in lines and stanzas. Like the poem you wrote in Chapter 15, these poems express ideas vividly, without unnecessary words. Using this information, write a poem of 15–25 lines for your classmates to read.

4. Historical fiction uses facts, events, or people from history as important parts of the story. The main character may help build a log cabin in the 1850s, for example, or may witness events of the American Revolution. Pick a historical period that interests you and use historical details to write a 300- to 400-word story. As with all your stories, make sure the story has a beginning, a middle, and an end; and make sure that it focuses on one conflict or problem.

# Unit 4  Reflections

How are you different as a writer now that you have completed this unit on literary writing? What new knowledge do you have? How is your writing stronger? What kinds of things could you work on to become even stronger as a literary writer? Use the following space to reflect on your work in this unit and to set goals for the future.

## Focus on Me: My Achievements as a Literary Writer

What I've learned about literary writing in this unit:

Ways my literary writing is stronger now:

Things I can do to practice my skills of literary writing:

THE
MYSTERY LOVERS'
BOOK CLUB

## Get to Know the Genre: Response to Literature

In English class, one of the most common forms of student writing is the response to literature. A **response to literature** examines a character, a theme, the plot, or another part of a story, novel, or poem. The purpose of writing a response to literature is to explain key ideas that you have about the work. A strong response to literature uses relevant examples and details from the work to help make the response clear.

To write an effective response to literature, pay close attention to the six traits of writing. These are the characteristics that make your writing strong and help your reader understand and feel interested in your ideas about literature.

# Six Traits of a **Response to Literature**

| Ideas | The topic is narrowed to a specific character, theme, or other aspect of the literary work. Each detail clearly relates. |
|---|---|
| Organization | The response has a beginning, a middle, and an end. Details follow a logical order. |
| Voice | The writer uses an objective, knowledgeable tone. |
| Word Choice | Vivid, accurate words are used. |
| Sentence Fluency | A variety of sentence types and structures creates a pleasing rhythm to the writing. |
| Conventions | Capitalization, spelling, punctuation, and grammar are correct. |

Real-World Example

Many responses to literature are written for a class or a test in school. Other responses are written for publication in magazines, journals, newspapers, Web sites, and other public sources. Janet S. Thompson, a librarian, wrote the following response to help readers decide whether they wanted to read *Shark Girl*, a novel about a girl who survives a shark attack. Thompson's response was published in the *School Library Journal*.

Don't think and then write it down. Think on paper.
—HARRY KEMELMAN
(American mystery writer, 1908–1996)

> **Ideas:** the author and title of the novel

BINGHAM, Kelly. **Shark Girl.** 276 pp. Candlewick. 2007.

Gr. 6–10—Jane, 15, is smart, good-looking, and the best artist in her school. After a shark attack at a local beach results in the amputation of her right arm, nothing is the same. Bingham's free-verse novel neatly accommodates the teen's loss; her dreams, anger, and frustration are explored as she rebelliously tries to adjust to her new circumstances. The main narrative is interspersed with news clippings, internal dialogue, and letters of support from other amputees, and even though Jane resists being part of that community, there are connections. Her voice is authentic and believable as both a teenager and victim. This engaging read will entice enthusiastic and reluctant readers; the drama of the shark attack will hook them, and Jane's inner journey will hold them till the end.—*Janet S. Thompson, Chicago Public Library*

> **Organization:** chronological order based on events in the book

> **Word choice:** specific nouns

> **Voice:** third-person point of view

> **Sentence fluency:** This compound sentence has three main clauses.

## Give It a Try: Examine the Real-World Example

Can you find additional examples of the traits of good writing in the model paragraph above? On separate paper, list three traits of writing. For each one, quote or describe an example from the model.

## Get Ready to Write

Now that you've explored the qualities of literary-response writing, you're ready to write some responses of your own. In the chapters that follow, you'll respond to a character in a story, a poem's theme, and a group of historical documents, and you'll also write about literature by examining a meaningful quotation. You'll use the stages of the writing process—prewriting, drafting, revising, editing, and publishing—and you'll be presented with models and mini-lessons along the way.

As you work through these chapters, you can enrich your understanding by trying the suggestions below. These tips will help you connect what you're learning in this unit to your own life and the world around you.

## LEARNING TIPS

- Collect interesting and inspiring quotations from songs, movies, friends, speeches, and literature. Choose your favorites and write personal responses to them.

- After watching a movie with friends, have a discussion in which you explain your responses to characters or themes in the movie.

- Watch for assignments in other classes that ask for your written response. For example, a history assignment may ask you to write a response to a description of ancient Rome. A science assignment may ask you to respond to a biography of Leonardo da Vinci or to the account of a scientific discovery.

# Respond to a Narrative

The next time your friends discuss a movie or television show, listen to what they say about the characters.

*"The main character is so funny. I know someone who has the same sense of humor!"*

*"The villain was truly evil, but I can understand why he did what he did."*

In the same way that you respond to characters in film and television, you can respond to characters in fiction. You might explain what their personality is like or how they changed.

Why write a response to a literary character? For one thing, you share your conclusions about the character, based on details you see in the story. In addition, you may help readers understand the story better or learn from the story. The table below explains key traits of a well-written response.

## Six Traits of a **Response to a Narrative**

| Ideas | The topic is narrowed to a specific character, theme, or other part of the literary work. Each detail clearly relates. |
|---|---|
| organization | The response has a beginning, a middle, and an end. Details follow a logical order. |
| voice | The writer uses an objective, knowledgeable tone. |
| word choice | Vivid, accurate words are used. |
| sentence Fluency | A variety of sentence types and structures creates a pleasing rhythm to the writing. |
| conventions | Capitalization, spelling, punctuation, and grammar are correct. |

In the response to literature below, the writer explains how and why a character changes over the course of a novel.

*That Summer* by Sarah Dessen tells the heartbreaking yet inspiring story of Haven's summer. Haven, a typical teenager, watches as everyone around her changes in ways that she does not like. Her parents have gotten divorced, and her dad is getting remarried. Her mom is having a midlife crisis. Her older sister is getting married to a boring guy. Even Haven's best friend is different after going to summer camp. Into the chaos of Haven's life comes Sumner, her sister's old boyfriend. Sumner reminds Haven of that summer when things were perfect, and the two become friends. Through Sumner, Haven clings to the past like a security blanket. But Sumner is not everything that Haven thought he was. When Haven learns the real reason why Sumner and her sister broke up, she has to let go of her idea of the perfect past and embrace her own future, whatever it holds.

## Give It a Try: Examine the Model Paragraph

Use the model paragraph above to answer the following questions. Write your answers on separate paper. Then explain your answers in a class discussion.

1. **Ideas.**
   a. What is the title of the work of literature?
   b. Who is the author of the work of literature?
   c. Who is the subject of this character sketch?
2. **Organization.** Explain the writer's method of organizing the paragraph.

3. **Voice and word choice.** List two words that express the writer's opinions about parts of the book.

4. **Sentence fluency.** Find and copy a *complex sentence* from the paragraph.

5. **Conventions.** In the model paragraph, the title of the book is printed in italic type. If you wrote this in handwriting, how would you show the title?

Now you'll write your own response to a story. Read the assignment carefully and follow the strategies and instructions for each stage of the writing process.

## Assignment

Choose a character from a story or novel you think your classmates would enjoy hearing about. Write a paragraph of 100–150 words in which you explain the character's personality *or* explain how the character changes during the narrative. Be sure to include

- the title of the work of literature
- the author of the work of literature
- the name of the character you are examining
- supporting examples from the narrative

**Analyze the Prompt.** Reread the assignment closely and answer the following questions. Write your answers on separate paper.

1. What is the purpose of this response to literature?
2. Who is the audience for this response to literature?
3. How long does the response need to be?

**Choose a Topic.** Make a list of stories and novels that you have enjoyed reading. Next to each title, write the name of a memorable character from that narrative. Which character has a personality that you would enjoy explaining? Which character changes in a noteworthy way?

Circle the name of the character who will be the focus of your character sketch.

**Gather Ideas and Details.** Use the following character map to gather ideas and details for your character sketch.

| | |
|---|---|
| Title and author of work | |
| Character's name | |
| His or her place in literature | |
| Age | |
| Personality | |
| Strengths | |
| Weaknesses | |
| Problems | |
| Response to problems | |
| Other details | |

**Organize Ideas and Details.** Use a beginning-middle-end table to organize the information to include in your paragraph. In the example table below, the writer has organized details for a paragraph about a character named Enid.

---

**Beginning**

Character: Enid
Title: *Taking Care of Terrific*
Author: Lois Lowry
Topic sentence: Enid learns to like things about herself.

---

**Middle**

Example 1: Enid babysits Tom. He has fun with her.
Example 2: Enid meets Hawk. He teaches her about the homeless.
Example 3: Enid helps the homeless people get rides on the swan
         boats.

---

**End**

Final thought: Enid is terrific because she makes people happy.

---

 Draft

When writing a response to literature, let your interest in the topic shine through. At the same time, use an objective, knowledgeable tone. A few strategies will help you do this.

- Use vivid yet accurate nouns and verbs. For example, write "heartbreaking yet inspiring" instead of "sad yet good."
- Use specific names rather than descriptions. For example, write "Tom Terrific" instead of "the little boy."

- Use the third-person point of view. For example, write "Enid is a terrific person," instead of "You will see that Enid is terrific."

**Write Your Response to Literature.** Write your one-paragraph response, using the beginning-middle-end table to guide you. In the following sample rough draft, the writer has placed check marks next to important parts of the paragraph. She also has jotted a few notes about revisions to do in the next stage of writing.

| Rough Draft | Writer's Notes for Revisions |
|---|---|
| The book that I read is *Taking Care of Terrific*. This is the story of Enid. She is fourteen years old. She doesn't like her name, but I like it okay. She doesn't like much of anything about herself. She takes care of Tom Terrific. Tom is four years old. Really his name is Joshua. But he wants to be called Tom Terrific. That was funny. They go to the Boston Public Garden. They meet some interesting people there. The people help Enid learn to like herself. One of these people plays the saxophone. This is a musical instrument. Another person is a bag lady. This means that she is homeless. Hawk tells Enid what being homeless means. Enid gives the homeless people a ride in the swan boats on the lake. Enid turns out to be a terrific person, even though she breaks the babysitting rules. She makes everyone around her happy. | Need to state the book's author.<br><br>Take out personal opinions.<br><br>Tell what this place is.<br><br>Tell his name.<br><br>Don't make a new point without explaining it. |

## Revise

At this point, you have the rough draft of your one-paragraph response. You may have jotted down some notes about things that need to be revised. Now it's time to make changes—large or small—to make the paragraph as strong as possible. For example, add sentence variety by combining sentences or adding introductory elements. Remove details that distract the reader from your purpose for writing. The checklist and rubric that follow will help you decide what changes to make to strengthen your paragraph.

**Revise Your Response to Literature.** Use the following checklist and the Response to Literature Rubric to guide your revision of your paragraph.

### Ideas
- ❏ Does the paragraph focus on either the character's personality or how the character changes during the narrative?
- ❏ Place a check mark next to the topic sentence where you introduce your main idea.
- ❏ Underline each detail that helps to explain your main idea. Remove any irrelevant details.

### Organization
- ❏ Did you arrange the details in a logical order, such as chronological order or order of importance?

### Voice
- ❏ Find three words that demonstrate an objective, knowledgeable tone. Write *voice* above them.
- ❏ Did you use the third-person point of view consistently?

### Word choice
- ❏ Circle three vivid, accurate words you used to make your ideas clear.

**Sentence fluency**

❏ Check that you used different kinds of sentence openers.

❏ Check that you used a few different sentence types (simple, compound, complex).

# Response to Literature Rubric

| | 4 Strong | 3 Effective | 2 Developing | 1 Beginning |
|---|---|---|---|---|
| **Ideas** | One topic is explained. Each detail clearly relates. | The topic is clear, but some details do not relate. | The writer is beginning to make the topic clear. | The topic is not clear. Most details do not relate. |
| **organization** | Details follow a logical order. | Most details follow a logical order. | Organization of details is awkward. | Details are in random order. |
| **voice** | The voice is interesting and reliable throughout the response. | The voice is interesting and reliable in most of the response. | The tone is interesting or reliable in a few sentences. | The tone is flat or mechanical, making it hard to connect to the writer. |
| **word choice** | Vivid, accurate words are used to express key ideas. | Vivid, accurate words are used to express most key ideas. | Vivid, accurate words are used to express one or two key ideas. | Vocabulary is limited. Some words are used incorrectly. |
| **sentence fluency** | A variety of sentence types is used in a pleasing rhythm. | A variety of sentence types is used, but some may be awkward. | Sentences are complete but are mostly short and simple. | Sentences are mostly short and simple or are incomplete. |
| **conventions** | Capitalization, spelling, punctuation, and grammar are correct. | A few errors in capitalization, spelling, punctuation, and grammar are present. | Errors in conventions do not prevent the reader from understanding. | Errors in conventions make it hard to understand the writing. |

## Edit

You have made the big revisions to your paragraph. Now it's time to focus on smaller changes, such as correcting mistakes in the conventions of writing. The following mini-lesson will help you identify—and use correctly—some words that are often confused with each other.

## Mini-Lesson: Spelling Words That Are Often Confused

Some of the most common spelling errors in English concern words that are easily confused with one another. For instance, you may write *there* when you should have written *their*. Or you may write *your* when you should have written *you're*. Most of these words are easy to confuse because they sound alike. To avoid these mistakes, become familiar with the following words and their meanings.

**Easily Confused Words, Table A**

| | |
|---|---|
| **accept**—to receive | **lose**—to be deprived of |
| **except**—to leave out | **loose**—not tight |
| **advice**—an offered suggestion | **their**—belonging to them |
| **advise**—to give advice to | **there**—a particular location |
| | **they're**—contraction of *they are* |
| **affect**—to act upon | **thorough**—complete |
| **effect**—a result | **through**—going from beginning to end |
| **close**—to shut | **to**—a preposition meaning movement toward something |
| **clothes**—garments; clothing | **too**—also |
| | **two**—the number 2 |
| **desert**—a dry wasteland | **your**—belonging to you |
| **dessert**—food (usually sweet) served at the end of a meal | **you're**—contraction of *you are* |

## Give It a Try: Identify Words That Are Easily Confused

Write definitions for each word in the following table.

### Easily Confused Words, Table B

| | |
|---|---|
| all ready— | emigrate— |
| already— | immigrate— |
| | |
| angel— | its— |
| angle— | it's— |
| | |
| attendance— | past— |
| attendants— | passed— |
| | |
| breath— | quiet— |
| breathe— | quit— |
| | quite— |
| principle— | |
| principal— | than— |
| | then— |

## Give It a Try: Edit for Easily Confused Words

Read the paragraph you wrote, looking closely at the spellings of words. Correct spelling errors. If you have confused one word with another, correct this spelling mistake.

**Edit Your Response to Literature.** Edit the revised copy of your character sketch. The following questions will help you decide what to change, remove, or leave in place.

### Conventions
- ❑ Did you underline or italicize the title of a novel?
- ❑ Did you place the title of a story in quotation marks?
- ❑ Did you use a comma when you began a sentence with an introductory element?

❑ Did you correct punctuation mistakes, either with a friend's help or by using a handbook?

❑ Did you correct spelling mistakes, either with a friend's help or by using a dictionary?

❑ Did you correct grammar mistakes, either with a friend's help or by using a grammar handbook?

## PUBLISH

**Presentation.** Prepare your paragraph for publication by neatly writing or typing the final, edited copy.

**Publish Your Paragraph.** Besides giving a copy of your paragraph to your teacher, you may want to publish your work in one of the following ways.

❑ Post a copy of the paragraph on your personal Web page or in a blog.

❑ Give a copy of the paragraph to a friend who would enjoy reading the short story or novel.

❑ Find (or create) a drawing or other image that helps to bring the character to life, such as a drawing of the character or an image of the book's cover. Get your teacher's permission to display your paragraph and the artwork on a class bulletin board.

# Evaluate Your Response to Literature

Your teacher will either assess your response, ask you to self-assess your response, or ask you to switch with a partner and assess each other's work.

# Evaluate the Model Response to Literature

Work with a partner to evaluate the following response to literature. Use the rubric on page 266 and write your score here: _____.
In a class discussion, explain the score that you gave.

### Terrific

Lois Lowry writes a lot of good books. One that I like a lot is *Taking Care of Terrific*. This is the story of Enid. She is fourteen years old. She doesn't like her name. She doesn't like much of anything about herself. She takes care of Tom Terrific. Tom is four years old. Really his name is Joshua. But he wants to be called Tom Terrific. They go to the Boston Public Garden, a public park with a lake in it. They meet some interesting people there. The people help Enid learn to like herself. One of these people plays the saxophone. His name is Hawk. This is a musical instrument. Another person is a bag lady. This means that she is homeless. Hawk tells Enid what being homeless means. Enid gives the homeless people a ride in the swan boats on the lake. Enid turns out to be a terrific person. She makes everyone around her happy.

# Respond to a Poem

You might be familiar with Aesop's fables—simple, short stories in which talking animals learn important life lessons. Each fable ends with a statement of the story's moral. For instance, in "The Fox and the Grapes" the moral is *It is easy to despise what you cannot have.* In "The Lion and the Mouse" the moral is *Little friends may prove great friends.*

A moral in one of Aesop's fables is much like a *theme* in other types of literature. A **theme**, as you know, is a lesson or message about life expressed by a story, poem, song, or other work. Usually, the writer expresses the theme indirectly through events, ideas, dialogue, figurative language, or other techniques. In this chapter, you will write a response to a poem in which you explain the poem's theme.

As with other forms of writing, a well-written response to literature includes the six traits of writing, as explained below.

## Six Traits of a **Response to a Poem**

| | |
|---|---|
| **Ideas** | The topic is narrowed to a specific theme or other part of the poem. Each detail clearly relates. |
| **organization** | The response has a beginning, a middle, and an end. Details follow a logical order. |
| **voice** | The writer uses an objective, knowledgeable tone. |
| **word choice** | The writer refers to specific images in the poem or quotes key words or phrases to make ideas clear. |
| **sentence fluency** | A variety of sentence types and structures creates a pleasing rhythm to the writing. |
| **conventions** | Capitalization, spelling, punctuation, and grammar are correct. |

Read the poem below. Then, in the passage that follows, read a response in which the writer discusses the poem's theme.

## She Dwelt Among the Untrodden Ways

William Wordsworth

She dwelt among the untrodden ways
Beside the springs of Dove,*
A Maid whom there were none to praise
And very few to love:

A violet by a mossy stone
Half hidden from the eye!
—Fair as a star, when only one
Is shining in the sky.

She lived unknown, and few could know
When Lucy ceased to be,
But she is in her grave, and, oh,
The difference to me!

*Dove: a river in England

### Love, Loss, and Lucy

William Wordsworth's poem "She Dwelt Among the Untrodden Ways" is about love and loss. The speaker tells about Lucy, a girl whom he loved but who has died. Through descriptions of Lucy, the poem's meaning becomes clear. A person does not have to be famous or popular to be valuable. The quietest, most unknown person can nevertheless mean all the world to someone.

To explain this theme, the speaker first tells how isolated and unknown Lucy was. He says, "She dwelt among the untrodden ways" and she was "Half hidden from the eye." He means that she kept to herself rather than being the center of a big social circle. Second, the speaker says that no one praised her, and only a few people loved her.

These descriptions could lead to the conclusion that Lucy was just a nobody, someone the world would never miss when she died. However, the speaker proves the opposite point. He says that even though few people noticed when she died, the loss of Lucy made a big difference to him. This "nobody" who attracted no praise and little love was, nevertheless, all the world to one person, and that is all that matters.

## Give It a Try: Examine the Model Passage

Use the model passage above to answer the following questions. Write your answers on separate paper. Then, in a class discussion, explain your answers.

1. **Ideas.** Copy the sentence from paragraph 1 in which the writer expresses the theme of the poem.
2. **Organization and word choice.** List transition words in paragraph 2 that draw attention to key points.
3. **Voice.** In this passage, does the writer use the first-person point of view or the third-person point of view? How do you know this?
4. **Sentence fluency.** Copy the second sentence in the passage. Underline the main clause once. Then underline each subordinate clause twice.
5. **Conventions.** Copy the sentence from paragraph 2 in which the writer quotes from the poem. Notice the placement of each quotation mark and punctuation mark.

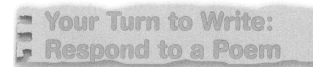

## Your Turn to Write: Respond to a Poem

Now you'll write your own response to a poem. Read the assignment carefully and follow the strategies and instructions for each stage of the writing process.

## Assignment

April is National Poetry Month, and a bookstore in your town is hosting a weekend of poetry readings in the store. You have been invited to read a response to a poem's theme. Choose one of the poems printed below. Then write a 200-word response in which you examine the poem's theme.

*choice 1*

### The Road Not Taken

Robert Frost

Two roads diverged in a yellow wood,
And sorry I could not travel both
And be one traveler, long I stood
And looked down one as far as I could
To where it bent in the undergrowth;

Then took the other, as just as fair,
And having perhaps the better claim,
Because it was grassy and wanted wear;
Though as for that, the passing there
Had worn them really about the same,

And both that morning equally lay
In leaves no step had trodden black.
Oh, I kept the first for another day!
Yet knowing how way leads on to way,
I doubted if I should ever come back.

I shall be telling this with a sigh
Somewhere ages and ages hence:
Two roads diverged in a wood, and I—
I took the one less traveled by,
And that has made all the difference.

*choice 2*

### Time Does Not Bring Relief; You All Have Lied

Edna St. Vincent Millay

Time does not bring relief; you all have lied
   Who told me time would ease me of my pain!
   I miss him in the weeping of the rain;
I want him at the shrinking of the tide;
The old snows melt from every mountain-side,
   And last year's leaves are smoke in every lane;
   But last year's bitter loving must remain
Heaped on my heart, and my old thoughts abide!
There are a hundred places where I fear
   To go,—so with his memory they brim!
And entering with relief some quiet place
Where never fell his foot or shone his face
I say, "There is no memory of him here!"
   And so stand stricken, so remembering him!

## Prewrite

**Analyze the Prompt.** Reread the assignment closely and answer the following questions. Write your answers on separate paper.

1. What is the purpose of this response to literature?
2. Who is the audience for this response to literature?
3. How long does the response need to be?

**Choose a Topic.** Carefully read both poems. Then choose one to write about.

**Gather Ideas and Details.** As your teacher directs, get together with other students who chose the same poem as you did. Gather ideas and details for your response to the poem by discussing the poem with one another. These sentence starters will help you.

This poem is mainly about . . .

The part I like best is . . .

The poet probably wants us to learn that . . .

I didn't understand the part about . . .

I really liked the way the poet said this . . .

A literary device [simile, metaphor, personification] that I see is . . .

A line in the poem that helps me identify the theme is . . .

**Organize Ideas and Details.** Plan the arrangement of ideas and details in your response. Create an outline using the following as a model. Write your information on a clean sheet of paper.

| Parts of Your Literary Response | Notes |
|---|---|
| **Beginning**<br>The poem's title is . . .<br>The author is . . .<br>My thesis is . . . | In the first paragraph, identify the name of the poem and the author.<br><br>Make a statement about the poem's theme that your essay will prove. |
| **Middle**<br>My first supporting detail is . . .<br>My second supporting detail is . . .<br>My third supporting detail is . . . | Include at least two supporting details. Refer to specific ideas in the poem, or quote key words or phrases, to illustrate your ideas. |
| **End**<br>My closing idea is . . . | Based on the evidence that you gave, restate the theme of the poem. |

Draft

Since your purpose for writing this response is to examine the poem's theme, be sure to state the theme of the poem. A theme, as you remember, is the life lesson that the poet wants to teach readers. In the model response that begins this chapter, the writer states the theme at the end of the first paragraph.

> The quietest, most unknown person can nevertheless mean all the world to someone.

A strong conclusion drives home the poem's theme by restating it in different words. In the model response, the writer restates the theme in this sentence:

> This "nobody" who attracted no praise and little love was, nevertheless, all the world to one person, and that is all that matters.

Notice that in the conclusion, the statement of the theme uses details from the essay. The word "nobody" refers to Lucy, and the topics of praise and love are from stanza 1 of the poem. The final clause, "that is all that matters," is the writer's own judgment on the theme.

**State a Theme of a Poem.** On separate paper, state a theme of the poem that you chose to write about.

**Write Your Response to a Poem.** Using your prewriting and the theme that you stated, write the first draft of your response to the poem. Be sure to
- ❏   include a beginning, a middle, and an end
- ❏   write using the third-person point of view
- ❏   refer to specific images in the poem, or quote specific words and phrases, to help make your ideas clear

> **T!p**   A poem may contain more than one theme, and these themes may
> be expressed in different ways. It's okay if you don't state a theme in
> exactly the same way as a classmate does. The important thing is that
> you explain your choice in the paragraph you write.

## Revise

Have you ever been talking to a friend and noticed a speck of
food stuck in his teeth? One minute you hear everything he says,
and the next minute all you can think about is the distracting
detail. Mistakes in writing are similar. Misspelled words, missing
punctuation marks, or incomplete sentences can hog your reader's attention so that they miss the important things you have to
say. Getting peer feedback on your writing can help bring some
of these distracting details to your attention. The following mini-
lesson explains.

## Mini-Lesson: Getting (and Giving) Helpful Feedback

One of the most helpful things you can do as a writer is to seek
feedback on your work in progress. A second pair of eyes may
see strengths and weaknesses that you've overlooked.

The key to getting (and giving) helpful feedback is to be
specific about what the reviewer should do. A request such as,
"Would you read this and tell me what you think?" is too vague.
Your reviewer is likely to say something like, "I liked it. Great
work!" This kind of response is good for the ego but not helpful
for improving a composition.

In contrast, a request such as, "Which sentence in this paragraph seems to be my topic sentence?" is specific. It will get you
specific feedback such as, "I think the second sentence is your
topic sentence" or "I couldn't find your topic sentence."

# Give It a Try: Get Feedback on Your Response to a Poem

Get out the draft of your response to a poem. Write down *three* specific questions to ask a peer reviewer. Here are some examples:

> Can you tell which sentence expresses the theme of the poem?
> Can you tell which is the topic sentence in paragraph 2?
> Would you rate the sentence fluency as pleasing, okay, or repetitive?

Now exchange drafts and questions with a classmate. If you responded to Robert Frost's poem, exchange drafts with someone who responded to Edna St. Vincent Millay's poem, and vice versa. On the draft you receive, write answers to the writer's questions. If necessary, underline sentences or circle words in the draft to help make your feedback clear. Finally, return the draft and your feedback to the writer.

**Revise Your Response to a Poem.** Revise the rough draft of your essay. Use the feedback you received and the following checklist and rubric to guide your revision.

## Ideas
- ☐ Place a check mark next to the sentence where you state the theme of the poem.
- ☐ Underline each detail you included to make the theme clear.

## Organization
- ☐ Check that you included a thesis statement, supporting points, and a conclusion.

## Voice

❏ Find three words that demonstrate your objective, knowledgeable tone. Write *voice* above them.

❏ Check that you used the third-person point of view consistently.

## Word choice

❏ Do you refer to specific ideas or images in the poem, or quote specific words, to help make your ideas clear? Add specific details if necessary.

❏ Circle two transition words you used to draw attention to your main points.

## Sentence fluency

❏ Check that you used different types of sentences (simple, compound, complex).

❏ Check that you used different kinds of sentence beginnings.

# Response to Poetry Rubric

| | 4<br>Strong | 3<br>Effective | 2<br>Developing | 1<br>Beginning |
|---|---|---|---|---|
| **Ideas** | One theme is explained. Each detail clearly relates. | The theme is clear, but some details do not relate. | The writer is beginning to make the theme clear. | The theme is not clear. Most details do not relate. |
| **organization** | The response has a clear beginning, middle, and end. | The beginning or ending is unclear. | The beginning or ending is missing. | The writer's thoughts are given in random order. |
| **voice** | The voice is objective and knowledgeable throughout the response. | The voice is objective and knowledgeable in most of the response. | The tone is objective and knowledgeable in one or two sentences. | The tone is preachy, careless, or otherwise not objective. |
| **word choice** | Vivid words and relevant quotes express key ideas. | Many vivid words, along with some basic ones, express key ideas. | One or two vivid words help to express a key idea. | Vocabulary is limited or does not clearly relate to the poem. |
| **sentence fluency** | A variety of sentence types is used in a pleasing rhythm. | A variety of sentence types is used, but some may be awkward. | Sentences are complete but are mostly short and simple. | Sentences are mostly short and simple or are incomplete. |
| **conventions** | Capitalization, spelling, punctuation, and grammar are correct. | Few errors in capitalization, spelling, punctuation, or grammar are present. | Errors in conventions do not prevent the reader from understanding. | Errors in conventions make it hard to understand the writing. |

# Edit

Use the following checklist to edit the revised copy of your response to a poem.

**Conventions**
- ❏ Did you capitalize each important word in the poem's title?
- ❏ Did you capitalize the poet's name?
- ❏ Did you use quotation marks to enclose the poet's exact words?
- ❏ Did you correct punctuation mistakes, either with a friend's help or by using a handbook?
- ❏ Did you correct spelling mistakes, either with a friend's help or by using a dictionary?
- ❏ Did you correct grammar mistakes, either with a friend's help or by using a grammar handbook?

## PUBLISH

**Presentation.** Prepare your essay for publication by neatly writing or typing the final, edited copy.

**Publish Your Essay.** Besides giving a copy of your essay to your teacher, you may want to publish your work in one of these ways.
- ❏ Create a video presentation by reading the poem and your response aloud while a friend films you. Post the video on a school Web site or a safe public Web site.
- ❏ In class, at home, or in a local bookstore, host a Poetry Response Party. Each participant should read a poem aloud and then read a one-paragraph response to the poem.
- ❏ Submit your response to a Web site that publishes the work of young people.
- ❏ Illustrate your response with a photograph or drawing, and share this with your teacher or classmates.

# Evaluate Your Response to a Poem

Your teacher will either assess your response, ask you to self-assess your response, or ask you to switch with a partner and assess each other's work.

# Evaluate a Model Response to a Poem

Work with a partner to evaluate the following model essay. Use the rubric on page 281 and write your score here: _____. In a class discussion, explain the score that you gave.

Poor, Sad Me

In William Wordsworth's "She Dwelt Among the Untrodden Ways," the speaker tells about Lucy. In doing so, he reveals more about himself than he does about Lucy. The poem shows that some people see others as valuable only in relation to themselves and not to the world at large.

First of all, the speaker seems more interested in being Lucy's sole admirer than in anything Lucy did, said, or felt. He seems self-satisfied that he alone has found her on the "untrodden ways." Second, the speaker writes a whole stanza about Lucy's beauty, which only *he* has noticed. She is a "half hidden" violet. She is a star in the sky––the only star, in fact. The speaker shows that he can ignore thousands of other people (excuse me, "stars") and pretend that there is only one in front of him and no one but he notices it.

Third, the speaker describes Lucy's death in terms of himself. He says that "few" people noticed when Lucy died, but he doesn't say if there was a funeral or what/who she left behind. His only thought is how her death makes *him* feel: "oh, / The difference to me!" He mourns the loss of Lucy because it is *his* loss, not because he knew her well enough to honor *her* life.

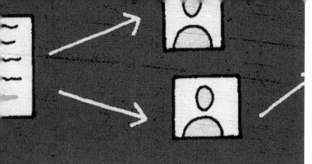

# Chapter 19

# Respond to a Document-Based Question

A **document-based question**, or **DBQ**, is based on two or more *primary sources* that relate to one another. A primary source is a firsthand account of an event. These are primary sources:

| | | |
|---|---|---|
| diaries | photographs | newspaper articles |
| journals | legal documents | receipts and other records |
| letters | speeches | maps |

The primary sources in a DBQ link to the same historical topic or period, such as the European Renaissance. Your purpose in responding to the documents is to explain how they relate or what they say as a group. To do this, you use a combination of information in the documents and your own knowledge. This chapter shows you how to write a strong response to a DBQ.

## Six Traits of a **Response to a DBQ**

| | |
|---|---|
| Ideas | The thesis links directly to the topic in the prompt. The writer uses supporting details from the documents and from previous knowledge. |
| organization | The response has a beginning, a middle, and an end.. |
| voice | The writer uses an objective, knowledgeable tone. |
| word choice | The writer refers to specific ideas in the documents or quotes key words or phrases to make his or her points clear to the reader. |
| sentence fluency | A variety of sentence types and structures creates a pleasing rhythm to the writing. |
| conventions | Direct quotations begin and end with quotation marks. Proper nouns are capitalized. Spelling, punctuation, and grammar are correct. |

In the essay below, the writer responds to two documents about the Irish Potato Famine, which occurred in Ireland between 1846 and 1850.

### The Irish Potato Famine

The Irish Potato Famine devastated Ireland during the years 1846—1850. Thousands of Irish died of starvation or from diseases they were too weak to recover from. Many more thousands emigrated to escape death, mostly to America. Within five years, Ireland lost an estimated one million people to death and another one million to emigration (Document 1). What caused this disastrous famine?

Before the famine, a large portion of the Irish population relied on potatoes as the main source of food. Then a potato blight ruined the potato crops for three years in a row. The blight caused the potatoes to rot while still in the ground. The crops were inedible.

Newspapers reported the desperation, pain, and suffering. For example, workers on a road project were too weak to work. A man, Mr. Marmion, said, "The unfed wretches have not energy enough to keep their blood in circulation, and they drop down from the united effects of cold and hunger--never to rise again" (Document 2). In another newspaper account, a Dr. Donovan says that people were "dropping in dozens" from starvation (Document 2). For Ireland, it was perhaps the worst disaster to ever hit the nation.

# Give It a Try: Examine the Model Essay

Work with a classmate to answer the following questions about the model essay on the previous page. Write your answers on separate paper. Then explain your answers in a class discussion.

1. **Ideas.** What historical event is the focus of this passage?
2. **Organization.** Identify the essay's beginning, middle, and end by drawing a circle around each part. Label each circle.
3. **Voice and word choice.** What do you think the writer's attitude toward the historical event is? How can you tell?
4. **Sentence fluency.** Why does the writer ask a question at the end of paragraph 1?
5. **Conventions.** Why does the writer place some words inside parentheses?

Your Turn to Write: Respond to a Document-Based Question

Now you'll write your own response to a DBQ. Read the assignment carefully and follow the strategies and instructions for each stage of the writing process.

# Assignment

**Historical Background** During the Industrial Revolution, many workers took jobs at factories. Many of these workers were children. Conditions at factories were often dirty and unsafe. For instance, on March 25, 1911, a fire broke out at the Triangle Shirtwaist Factory in New York City. One hundred forty-six garment workers lost their lives in the disaster.

**Writing Prompt** Write a 200-word essay for your classmates to read. Explain what working conditions were like in some factories during the Industrial Revolution. Use information from at least two of the documents and your own knowledge of the Industrial Revolution.

## Document 1: **First-Person Accounts from Factory Workers**

**Clara Lemlich:**

First let me tell you something about the way we work and what we are paid. There are two kinds of work—regular, that is salary work, and piecework. The regular work pays about $6 a week and the girls have to be at their machines at 7 o'clock in the morning and they stay at them until 8 o'clock at night, with just one-half hour for lunch in that time. . . .

The shops are unsanitary—that's the word that is generally used, but there ought to be a worse one used. Whenever we tear or damage any of the goods we sew on, or whenever it is found damaged after we are through with it, whether we have done it or not, we are charged for the piece and sometimes for a whole yard of the material.

**Sadie Frowne:**

My name is Sadie Frowne. I work in Allen Street (Manhattan) in what they call a sweatshop. I am new at the work and the foreman scolds me a great deal. I get up at half-past five o'clock every morning and make myself a cup of coffee on the oil stove. I eat a bit of bread and perhaps some fruit and then go to work. Often I get there soon after six o'clock so as to be in good time, though the factory does not open till seven. . . .

The machines go like mad all day because the faster you work the more money you get. Sometimes in my haste I get my finger caught and the needle goes right through it. It goes so quick, though, that it does not hurt much. I bind the finger up with a piece of cotton and go on working. We all have accidents like that.

## Document 2: **Newspaper Article**

### 141 Men and Girls Die in Shirtwaist Factory Fire; Trapped High Up in Washington Place Building; Street Strewn with Bodies; Piles of Dead Inside

Three stories of a ten-floor building at the corner of Greene Street and Washington Place were burned yesterday, and while the fire was going on 141 young men and women— a least 125 of them mere girls—were burned to death or killed by jumping to the pavement below. . . .

Most of the victims were suffocated or burned to death within the building, but some who fought their way to the windows and leaped met death as surely, but perhaps more quickly, on the pavements below. . . .

Nothing like it has been seen in New York since the burning of the *General Slocum*.* The fire was practically all over in half an hour. It was confined to three floors—the eighth, ninth, and tenth of the building. But it was the most murderous fire that New York has seen in many years.

\* *General Slocum*: a ferry that caught fire in 1904; more than 1,000 passengers died

### Document 3: Photograph

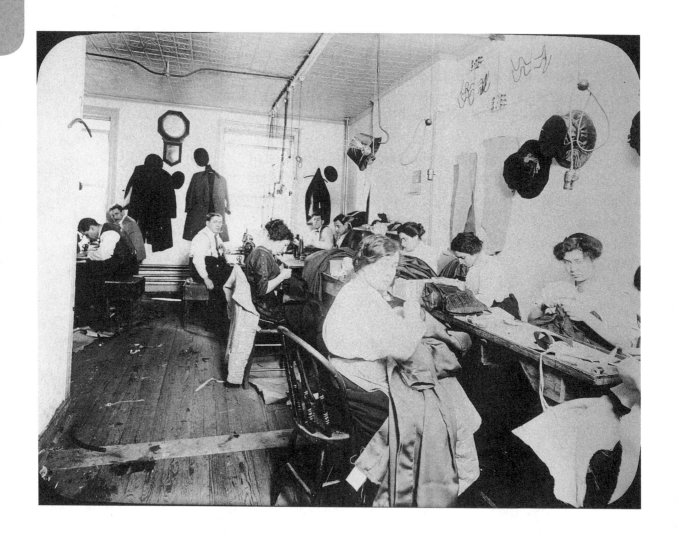

 Prewrite

**Analyze the Prompt.** Use the assignment on page 287 to answer the questions in the paragraphs that follow.

A document-based question usually has three main sections. First, a few sentences give background information on the theme or subject of the DBQ. In the assignment on page 287, this information is included under the heading "Historical Background."

1. According to the background, what is the subject of this DBQ?

   After the background, a section gives you a topic for your written response. In the assignment on page 287, this section is called "Writing Prompt." It might also be called Task.

2. According to the prompt

   **a.** what is the purpose of this essay?

   **b.** who is the audience for this essay?

   **c.** how long does the essay need to be?

   **d.** how many primary sources must you use?

   Finally, you'll see the documents. These are primary sources that you must use when writing your response.

3. Write the titles of the primary sources in this DBQ.

**Read the Documents.** Reading and understanding the documents is your next step in preparing to write your response. Unless you are writing for a test, you can discuss the documents with your teacher and classmates. In addition, you can use these tips:

- **Read each document more than once.** First, read to get the big picture. What's happening? What is (are) the writer's main point(s)? Next, read to understand more completely. Figure out the areas that confused you during your first reading. Finally, read again to tie it all together in your mind.

- **Mark unfamiliar words and find out their meanings.**

- **Identify the writer's strategy for organizing information.** Did the writer use chronological order? A cause-and-effect pattern? A compare-and-contrast pattern? A list of reasons in order of importance? If you know how ideas are organized, you can better figure out the challenging parts.

- **Summarize. In a sentence or two, restate the writer's main idea.** Your summary could begin, "He's basically saying that . . ." or "She wants people to know/think that. . . ."

**Read the Documents in the DBQ.** Use the reading tips on the previous page to read and understand the documents in the DBQ. Then share your ideas in a class discussion. These sentence starters may help you get the discussion started.

Clara Lemlich's account gives details about . . .
Sadie Frowne's account gives details about . . .
The purpose of the newspaper article is to . . .
The photograph shows . . .
One of the unfamiliar words I looked up is . . .
[Name a source] uses the organization method of . . .
One question I still have is . . .

**Gather Ideas and Details.** In a response to a DBQ, you must use information from the documents plus your own knowledge. Gather together this information by using the table below. Continue on separate paper if necessary.

| My purpose for writing: _____ | | |
|---|---|---|
| What the Documents Say | What I Know | What I Can Conclude Based on Both Sets of Information |
| | | |

**Organize Ideas and Details.** Plan the arrangement of ideas and details in your response. Create an outline using the following model. Write your information on separate paper.

| Parts of Your Essay | In This Part You Should . . . |
|---|---|
| **Beginning**<br>My topic is . . .<br>The author is . . .<br>My thesis is . . . | Make a statement about working conditions in factories during the Industrial Revolution. This statement is what your essay will explain or prove. |
| **Middle**<br>My first supporting detail is . . .<br>My second supporting detail is . . .<br>My third supporting detail is . . . | Prove your thesis. Use supporting examples from at least two of the documents, plus your own knowledge and conclusions. |
| **End**<br>My closing idea is . . . | Summarize your information in a closing statement about your thesis |

## Draft

By now, you have put a great deal of effort into understanding the DBQ and the documents in the DBQ. Moreover, you have worked to gather and organize ideas. Take a moment to appreciate how far you've come in preparing your response! You will benefit from all your preparation now that it's time to write your response.

As you write, make sure that you use quotations accurately. The following mini-lesson explains how to use quotations from documents in a DBQ.

# Mini-Lesson: Using Quotations

A response to a DBQ is not a summary of the documents in the DBQ. Instead, the response is made up of your ideas and conclusions about information in the documents. To show how your ideas link to the documents, you can quote key words or phrases from the sources.

In the paragraph about the Irish Potato Famine, here is how the writer used a quotation.

> In another newspaper account, a Dr. Donovan says that people were "dropping in dozens" from starvation (Document 2).

Notice three things about the use of the quotation.

- The writer identifies who is speaking or writing (Dr. Donovan).
- The writer places quotation marks around the quoted words.
- The writer tells which document the quote comes from (Document 2).

## Give It a Try: Write Sentences That Use Quotations

Skim the documents in the DBQ. Choose three words or phrases that are especially vivid or well phrased *and* that link to your ideas for your response. On separate paper, write three sentences in which you quote words or phrases from a document. In each sentence, be sure to identify the writer or speaker, use quotation marks, and identify the document number. Your teacher may ask you to work with a partner to complete this activity.

**Write Your Response to a DBQ.** Use your prewriting, organization table, and sentences from the mini-lesson to write the first draft of your response to the DBQ. Be sure to

❑ include a beginning, a middle, and an end
❑ write using the third-person point of view
❑ use examples and quotations to make your ideas clear

## Revise

**Get Feedback on Your Response to a DBQ.** Read the draft of your response. Write down *three* specific requests for a peer reviewer. Here are some examples:

Please circle my thesis statement.

Can you tell whether each supporting detail comes from a document or from my own knowledge?

What is the strongest sentence or idea in my essay?

Please write a question mark next to details that don't seem to relate to the topic.

Now exchange drafts and questions with a classmate. On the draft you receive, write answers to the writer's questions. If necessary, underline sentences or circle words in the draft to help make your feedback clear. Finally, return the draft and your feedback to the writer.

**Revise Your Response to a DBQ.** Revise the rough draft of your essay. Use the feedback you received and the following checklist and rubric to guide you.

### Ideas
❑ Reread the prompt. Check that your response addresses the prompt.
❑ Check that you used details from the documents *and* your own knowledge to prove your thesis.

### Organization
❑ Did you include a thesis statement, supporting sentences, and a conclusion?

### Voice
❑ Did you use an objective, knowledgeable tone?
❑ Did you use the third-person point of view consistently?

### Word choice
❑ Underline three places where you referred to specific ideas or images in the documents, or quoted specific words, to help make your ideas clear.

### Sentence fluency
❑ Did you use different types of sentences (simple, compound, complex)?
❑ Did you use different kinds of sentence beginnings?

# Response to a DBQ Rubric

|  | 4<br>Strong | 3<br>Effective | 2<br>Developing | 1<br>Beginning |
|---|---|---|---|---|
| **Ideas** | The thesis links to the prompt. Details come from the documents and the writer's knowledge. | The thesis links to the prompt but is weak. Most details come from the documents and the writer's knowledge. | No clear thesis. Details are all from either the documents or the writer's knowledge. | No thesis. The essay is not focused on one topic or does not relate to the prompt. |
| **organization** | The essay has a clear beginning, middle, and end. | The beginning or ending is unclear. | The beginning or ending is missing. | The writer's thoughts are given in random order. |
| **voice** | The voice is objective and knowledgeable throughout the response. | The voice is objective and knowledgeable in most of the response. | The tone is objective and knowledgeable in one or two sentences. | The tone is goofy, sarcastic, or otherwise not objective. |
| **word choice** | Vivid words and relevant quotes express key ideas. | Many vivid words, along with some basic ones, express key ideas. | One or two vivid words help to express a key idea. | Vocabulary is limited. Some words are used incorrectly. |
| **sentence fluency** | A variety of sentence types is used in a pleasing rhythm. | A variety of sentence types is used, but some may be awkward. | Sentences are complete but are mostly short and simple. | Sentences are mostly short and simple or are incomplete. |
| **conventions** | Capitalization, spelling, punctuation, and grammar are correct. | Few errors in capitalization, spelling, punctuation, or grammar are present. | Errors in conventions do not prevent the reader from understanding. | Errors in conventions make it hard to understand the writing. |

## Edit

Edit your essay. The following questions will help.

**Conventions**
❏ Did you capitalize proper nouns?
❏ Did you use quotation marks to enclose words taken from a document?
❏ Did you use parentheses to enclose the document citation, like this: (Document 1)?
❏ Did you correct punctuation mistakes, either with a friend's help or by using a handbook?
❏ Did you correct spelling mistakes, either with a friend's help or by using a dictionary?
❏ Did you correct grammar mistakes, either with a friend's help or by using a grammar handbook?

## PUBLISH

**Presentation.** Prepare your essay for publication by neatly writing or typing the final, edited copy.

**Publish Your Essay.** Besides giving a copy of your essay to your teacher, you may want to publish your work in one of the following ways.
❏ Create a Web page to give factual information on your topic. Include your essay as the main feature and include links to other reliable Web sites about the topic.
❏ Read your paragraph to a younger student who would enjoy learning about the Industrial Revolution.
❏ E-mail a copy of your essay to friends or family members. Tell them why you think they would be interested in your ideas.

# Evaluate Your Response to a DBQ

Your teacher will either assess your response, ask you to self-assess your response, or ask you to switch with a partner and assess each other's work.

# Evaluate the Model Response to a DBQ

Work with a partner to evaluate the model essay about the Irish Potato Famine, on page 286. Use the rubric on page 297 and write your score here: _____. In a class discussion, explain the score that you gave.

# Test Writing:
# The Critical-Lens Essay

What's your favorite inspirational quotation? Your favorite movie tagline? Your favorite line from a song? These little sentences have a way of summing up big ideas, and they speak to different people in different ways. For example, what do these quotations mean to you? Do you agree or disagree with the message of each one?

"To escape criticism—say nothing, do nothing, be nothing."
—Elbert Hubbard
"No pain, no gain."
—proverb

On a test, you may be asked to write a response to a quotation like the ones listed above. This kind of response is often called a response to a critical-lens quotation. A **critical lens** is tool for examining life or literature. It gives you a frame of reference for talking about a truth. This chapter explains how to write a response to a critical-lens quotation.

## Six Traits of a **Critical-Lens Essay**

| Ideas | The writer interprets the quotation, agrees or disagrees with it, and explains it using examples from literature. |
|---|---|
| organization | The response has a beginning, a middle, and an end. Details follow a logical order. |
| voice | The writer uses an objective, knowledgeable tone. |
| word choice | Vivid, accurate words are used. |
| sentence fluency | A variety of sentence types and structures creates a pleasing rhythm to the writing. |
| conventions | Capitalization, spelling, punctuation, and grammar are correct. |

# Preparing to Write Your Test Essay

A prompt for a critical-lens response has two or three parts: your assignment, the critical-lens quotation, and (sometimes) a list of reminders or guidelines. Here is an example of a critical-lens prompt.

---

**Instructions**

You have 25 minutes to complete the written composition. Read the prompt below. Then use separate paper to plan and draft your composition. Only your draft will be scored.

**Writing Prompt**

Write an essay in which you discuss two works of literature from the perspective of the critical-lens quotation.
In your essay,

- give your interpretation of the quotation
- agree or disagree with the quotation
- support your opinion using details from two works of literature

**Critical Lens**

"Don't judge a book by its cover."
   —American proverb

**Remember to**

- state the titles and authors of the works of literature you discuss
- organize your ideas in a logical way
- follow the conventions of capitalization, spelling, punctuation, and grammar

---

## 1. Study the Prompt

Before you begin to write your essay, take a few moments to study the prompt. Answer these important questions:

a. **What is the purpose of the essay?** The writing prompt list three things that you must include in your response. List them on separate paper.

b. **What should you write about?** The writing prompt gives you a critical-lens quotation to respond to. Copy the quotation on your paper.

c. **How much time do you have to write?** According to the prompt, how much time is allowed for writing this response? Write it down.

d. **What other instructions are stated?** According to the prompt, what are three things the writer should remember to do? List them on your paper.

## 2. Plan Your Time

After studying the prompt, make a quick plan for how to use your time. If you have 25 minutes in which to write the test, you could use your time as follows:

5–7 minutes:     Study the prompt and complete the prewriting.

13–15 minutes: Write the essay.

5 minutes:         Revise and edit the essay.

## 3. Prewrite

During your prewriting time, gather and organize ideas. A table with a separate space for each part of the writing task is useful. It helps you gather ideas for the three parts of your response.

On the next page is an example of how a writer used a task table to gather and organize ideas about the critical-lens quotation in the sample prompt.

## Task Table

Task 1: Interpret the quote.

Don't form an opinion about someone or something based on appearances alone.

---

Task 2: Agree or disagree.

I agree.

Task 3: Give 2 examples from literature.

In <u>To Kill a Mockingbird</u> by Harper Lee, a black man is accused of a crime he really didn't commit. However, most residents of the 1930s town judge the man by his appearance—the fact that he is black—and assume he committed the crime. Atticus Finch defends Tom Robinson and proves that you shouldn't judge a book (or person) by its cover.

In <u>The Pigman</u> by Paul Zindel, John and Lorraine are teenagers who play pranks on people. They play a prank on Mr. Pignati because they think he is a foolish person. They jokingly call him the Pigman. They are judging him by first impressions, or appearances. In reality, as they learn, he is kind and generous and not foolish at all.

The table above is useful not just for gathering ideas but for organizing your response, too. In your essay, include the ideas in the order in which you wrote them in the table (Task 1, Task 2, Task 3). Then, to conclude the essay, write a sentence that restates your interpretation of the quote, using different words this time.

**T!p** Different people will interpret a quote differently, and some people may disagree with a quote that others agree with. What's important is that you support your interpretation with examples from literature.

# Writing Your Test Essay

After prewriting, move on to the writing stage. Keep these important tips in mind.

- Use your prewriting work to guide you. It's okay if you change a detail or two as you write the essay. However, don't stray too much from your plan, or you may create a disorganized mess.
- Review the "Remember to" section in the writing prompt and follow the reminders.
- Write neatly and leave space on the page for writing revisions. You can do this by leaving at least a one-inch margin all around, or by double-spacing your response.

TOOLKIT

For organizing a response to a critical-lens quotation, useful strategies include
- a task table
- an outline
- a beginning-middle-end table

T!p   Give your response a title. To create an effective title, you could state the theme of the quotation ("First Impressions") or use a key phrase from your response ("Refuse to Judge").

The model paragraph below is the introduction to an essay responding to a critical-lens quotation. Notice that the writer includes four important ingredients, as listed in the column to the right of the paragraph.

| Introductory Paragraph | Important Ingredients |
|---|---|
| An American proverb offers the advice, "Don't judge a book by its cover." In other words, do not jump to conclusions about a person based on your first impressions. Instead, get to know the person for who he or she truly is. As examples from *To Kill a Mockingbird* and *Pigman* show, the proverb is wise advice. | 1. the quotation<br>2. an interpretation of the quotation<br>3. an introduction of the examples from literature<br>4. a statement of agreement or disagreement with the quotation |

## Polishing Your Test Essay

Save approximately five minutes to use for polishing your response. Revise sentences, add or remove details, and correct mistakes in the conventions of writing. Taking the time to do this is useful for several reasons.

- It helps you show careful consideration of *all* six traits of writing.
- It makes ideas clear for your reader.
- It helps your reader connect with your response.

## Evaluating a Response to a Critical-Lens Quotation

When a teacher evaluates your response to a critical-lens quotation, he or she will check to be sure that you

- **wrote to the prompt.** This means that you included the three parts of the writing task. It also means that you did not include unrelated details, such as personal experiences.
- **included relevant details in an organized manner.** This means that you used examples from literature that clearly relate to your interpretation of the quotation. It also means that you arranged ideas in a clear, logical way.
- **paid careful attention to the conventions of capitalization, spelling, punctuation, and grammar.**

The following rubric shows guidelines for evaluating a response to a critical-lens quotation.

# Response to a Critical-Lens Quotation Rubric

| | 4<br>Strong | 3<br>Effective | 2<br>Developing | 1<br>Beginning |
|---|---|---|---|---|
| ideas | The writer wrote to the prompt. Each detail clearly relates. | The writer wrote to the prompt, but a few details do not relate. | The writer included some details relating to the prompt. | The writer did not write to the prompt. |
| organization | Information is arranged logically. | Most information is arranged logically. | Organization of information is awkward. | Information is included in random order. |
| voice | The writing style helps the reader connect to the response. | The writing style of some parts draws the reader in. | The writing style of one or two sentences draws the reader in. | Writing is mechanical, making it hard for readers to connect. |
| word choice | Most key words are vivid. Most words are used accurately. | A few vivid words are used. Most words are used accurately. | One or two vivid words are used. Vocabulary is limited. | Vocabulary is limited and difficult to understand. |
| sentence fluency | A variety of sentence types is used in a pleasing rhythm. | A variety of sentence types is used, but some may be awkward. | Sentences are complete but are mostly short and simple. | Sentences are mostly of one type or are incomplete. |
| conventions | Few errors in capitalization, spelling, punctuation, or grammar are present. | Several errors in capitalization, spelling, punctuation, or grammar are present. | Errors in capitalization, spelling, punctuation, and grammar do not prevent understanding. | Errors in capitalization, spelling, punctuation, and grammar prevent understanding. |

# Evaluate a Model Critical-Lens Test Essay

Work with a partner to evaluate the following response to a critical-lens quotation. Use the rubric on page 307 and write your score here: _____. In a class discussion, explain the score that you gave.

## Refuse to Judge

An American proverb offers the advise, Don't judge a book by its cover. In other words, do not jump to conclusions about a person based on your first impressions. Instead, get to know the person for who he or she truly is. As examples from To Kill a Mockingbird and The Pigman show, the proverb is wise advice.

To Kill a Mockingbird by Harper Lee is set in a small American town in the 1930s. In this town, most white people are prejudiced against black people. They judged people by their "covers": the color of their skin. Tom Robinson, a black man, is accused of raping a white woman. Because he is black, most people assume he did it. During the trial, the reader can see that the accuser, Mayella, is lying about Tom. Unfortunately, the jury convicts Tom anyway. The story shows how unfair, unjust, and damaging it can be to judge a book by its cover.

Similarly, The Pigman by Paul Zindel shows why it is wise not to judge a book by its cover. John and Lorraine, two teenagers, like to make prank telephone calls. One day they dial a random phone number and get Mr. Pignati. They tell him they are collecting money for a charity. When he offers to donate ten dollars, they assume he is a foolish, stupid man. However, After getting to know Mr. Pignati, they discover that he is a kind and generous person who is simply lonely. They develop a deep friendship with Mr. Pignati, Which they would have missed out on if they had not looked past the "cover."

As Tom Robinson and Mr. Pignati show, first impressions of a person can be incorrect. First impressions can be a reflection of your own prejudice or your own problems. By refuseing to judge a book, or person, by first impressions, you open yourself up to the possibility of justice and friendship.

# Write a Critical-Lens Test Essay

Try writing a response to a critical-lens quotation in a testlike setting. Respond to the writing prompt below.

---

**Instructions**

You have 25 minutes to complete the written composition. Read the prompt below. Then use separate paper to plan and draft your composition. Only your draft will be scored.

**Writing Prompt**

Write an essay in which you discuss two works of literature from the perspective of the critical-lens quotation. In your essay,

- give your interpretation of the quotation
- agree or disagree with the quotation
- support your opinion using details from two works of literature

**Critical Lens**

"All that glitters is not gold."
    —American proverb

**Remember to**

- state the titles and authors of the works of literature you discuss
- organize your ideas in a logical way
- follow the conventions of capitalization, spelling, punctuation, and grammar

---

Unit 5

# Response to Literature Wrap-Up

The activities and information in these pages will help you continue to strengthen your skills of writing responses to literature. In You Be the Judge, use the Response to Literature Rubric to evaluate a student's work. The Ideas for Writing are additional writing prompts you can use for practice. And finally, in the Unit 5 Reflections, you can list important ideas you have learned in this unit and set goals for future learning.

## You Be the Judge

Use what you've learned about the traits of writing to evaluate a student's response to literature. First, review the traits of writing on page 256. Next, read the student's work printed below. Finally, in the rubric that follows, assign the work a score for each writing trait. In the space provided, explain each score that you assign.

**Soul Surfer**

by Libby S., Omaha, NE

*Soul Surfer: A True Story of Faith, Family, and Fighting to Get Back on the Board* by Bethany Hamilton

Bethany Hamilton was born into a family of avid surfers. She has felt a unique and passionate love for the sport of surfing ever since she first got on board when she was a toddler. Bethany had always dreamed of becoming a professional surfer since she first started competing when she was only seven years old. She had everything going for her; wonderful friends, a great sponsor, and a loving and supportive family behind her. Then one day, something tragic happened.

It was Halloween morning in 2003. Bethany was surfing with her best friend Alana and the waves weren't very big. As Bethany lay on her board, soaking up the beautiful Hawaiian sun, she let her arm dangle in the water. All of a sudden she felt a tug and before she knew it, the water around her was red and a shark had her arm. Bethany and the people close to her were afraid that her surfing career was over.

Soul Surfer is an autobiography about Bethany Hamilton. In the book, you get to read about Bethany's life before, during, and after her tragic attack. It is a story of bravery, faith, and love that a thirteen-year-old girl experienced when her life was changed forever. I think Bethany told her story extremely well in this book, and it really made me feel close to her. Bethany writes about her true love for surfing and her struggle to become the best she could be. Soul Surfer is a book that will catch your attention from the very first page. It makes you realize that you should never give up. Bethany is now one of the top surfers competing, and she has only one arm. She still has her friends, sponsor, and of course her family and she has let nothing stop her.

I think that Soul Surfer is a truly wonderful and exciting story, and I would recommend it to any of my friends. Although this book is a good choice for anybody, I think that girls about 12–16 would enjoy Soul Surfer the most. Bethany's story has really helped many people open their eyes and see what you can accomplish when you try hard. I think this is an excellent book and if you want to read a book that is inspiring but not sappy, Soul Surfer could just be the book for you.

# Response to Literature Rubric

| | 4<br>**Strong** | 3<br>**Effective** | 2<br>**Developing** | 1<br>**Beginning** |
|---|---|---|---|---|
| **Ideas**<br>Score_____ | *explanation:* | | | |
| **organization**<br>Score_____ | *explanation:* | | | |
| **voice**<br>Score_____ | *explanation:* | | | |
| **word choice**<br>Score_____ | *explanation:* | | | |
| **sentence fluency**<br>Score_____ | *explanation:* | | | |
| **conventions**<br>Score_____ | *explanation:* | | | |

## Ideas for Writing

The assignments that follow will give you additional practice with literature response. Your teacher may choose one or let you pick one that's most interesting to you.

1. With a friend, choose a poem to which you both feel a strong reaction, positive or negative. On your own, each of you should write a 150-word response to the poem's theme, characters, or plot. Then, with your friend, examine both of your responses.

How were your responses similar? How were they different? Why do you think people have different responses to the same poem? With your teacher's permission, summarize your findings in a short presentation to your class.

2. Write a letter to an author explaining your response to a particular work that he or she wrote. In your letter, be sure to include

   - a beginning in which you identify the title of the work and the focus of your response

   - a middle in which you give examples from the work to support your response; you might also ask a question about the work that you were unable to answer

   - an ending in which you give a final thought about the work

   Your letter should be approximately 300 words long.

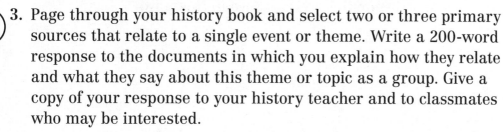

3. Page through your history book and select two or three primary sources that relate to a single event or theme. Write a 200-word response to the documents in which you explain how they relate and what they say about this theme or topic as a group. Give a copy of your response to your history teacher and to classmates who may be interested.

4. A Chinese proverb says, "If you get up one more time than you fall, you will make it through." Write a 350-word essay in which you explain the meaning of this proverb and discuss how you can apply the statement to characters from two different works of literature that you have read.

# Unit 5 Reflections

How are you different as a writer now that you have completed this unit on writing responses to literature? What new knowledge do you have? How is your writing stronger? What kinds of things could you work on to make your responses to literature even more effective? Use the following space to reflect on your work in this unit and to set goals for the future.

## Focus on Me: My Achievements in Writing Responses to Literature

What I've learned about responding to literature in this unit:




Ways my writing is stronger now:




Things I can do to practice my skills of responding to literature:

# Conventions Handbook

## Sentences

**active voice**   In a sentence written in active voice, the subject performs the action of the verb. Example: *Hannah cooked dinner.*

**comma splice**   Two or more sentences joined with only a comma.

**complex sentence**   A sentence containing one main clause and at least one subordinate clause.

**compound sentence**   A sentence containing two or more main clauses and no subordinate clauses.

**compound-complex sentence**   A sentence containing at least two main clauses and at least one subordinate clause.

**fragment**   A word group punctuated as a sentence yet lacking a subject, a verb, or both.

**run-on**   Two or more sentences run together without punctuation or a conjunction between them.

**passive voice**   In a sentence written in passive voice, the subject is acted upon; it receives the action of the verb. Example: *Dinner was cooked by Hannah.*

**simple sentence**   A sentence containing one subject and one verb (one main clause).

## The Eight Parts of Speech

**adjective**   Part of speech used to modify a noun or a pronoun.

**adverb**   Part of speech used to modify a verb, an adjective, or another adverb.

**conjunction**   Part of speech used to link words, phrases, clauses, or sentences.

**interjection**   Part of speech used to express sudden, strong feeling. It usually stands alone before a sentence.

**noun**   Part of speech that names a person, place, thing, or idea.

**preposition**   Part of speech that shows the relationship between its object(s) and another word in the sentence.

**pronoun**   Part of speech that takes the place of a noun in a sentence.

**verb**   Part of speech that expresses action or links the subject to another word in the sentence.

## How Words Work in Sentences

**agreement**   The subject and its verb are both expressed in the same number (singular or plural); a pronoun and its antecedent are both expressed in the same number and gender (male, female, or neuter).

**alliteration** The repetition of consonant sounds at the beginnings of words, as in *Holding hands in hot, hot sun*.

**antecedent**   The word or word group to which a pronoun refers.

**appositive**   A word or phrase that identifies or renames a noun or pronoun. An appositive follows the word it renames and is set off by commas.

**clause**   A related sequence of words that has a subject and a predicate. A *main clause* can stand alone as a sentence, but a *subordinate clause* cannot stand alone as a complete sentence.

**degrees of comparison**   The degrees of comparison are the *positive degree*, used to modify one thing (e.g., *fast*); the *comparative degree*, used to modify two things (*faster*); and the *superlative degree*, used to modify more than two things (*fastest*).

**direct object**   A noun that receives the action of a verb.

**double negative**   The use of more than one "no" word in a sentence, as in *I don't know nothing*.

**indirect object**   A noun that is indirectly affected by the action of the verb.

**irregular verb**   A verb that forms its past and past participles by changing the spelling of the word, but not by adding -*d* or -*ed*. Examples include *run, ran, has run* and *eat, ate, has eaten*.

**metaphor**   A figure of speech that makes a comparison indirectly by saying that one thing *is* the other thing. Example: *His fingers were thick sausages*.

**modifier**   A word, phrase, or clause that describes a word or word group. Modifiers are either adjectives or adverbs.

**object of a preposition**   The noun that a preposition links to another word in the sentence.

**onomatopoeia** The use of words to represent the sounds they describe, as in *pop*, *meow*, and *boom*.

**personification**   A figure of speech in which nonhuman things are given human qualities. Example: *The moon smiled down at the Earth.*

**phrase**   A related sequence of words that does not have a subject and/or a predicate and that is used as a single part of speech.

**predicate**   The part of a sentence that says something about the subject.

**regular verb**   A verb that forms its past and past participles by adding *-d* or *-ed* to the present-tense form. Examples include *help*, *helped*, *has helped* and *smile*, *smiled*, *has smiled*.

**rhyme**   The use of the same sound at the ends of words, especially words that end lines in a poem. The words *drink* and *think* rhyme.

**simile**   A figure of speech that makes a comparison by using the word *like*, *as*, or *than*. Example: *His fingers were thick **as** sausages.*

**subject**   The word or word group about which the predicate says something.

**tense**   Used in reference to a verb, indicates the time of the action or of the state of being (past, present, future).

**transition**   A word or phrase that connects two ideas, sentences, or paragraphs in a written work. Examples include *first*, *second*, *in addition*, and *therefore*.

**verb**   Part of speech that expresses action or links the subject to another word in the sentence. The verb is part of the predicate in a sentence.

## Punctuation

**apostrophe**   Used to form contractions and possessives.

**colon**   Used to call attention to what follows, such as when the first clause in a sentence announces a second clause or a list, often with the words *the following*. Used to separate the hour and minutes in written time. Used after the salutation in a business letter. Used to separate the city and the publisher in a bibliographic entry.

**comma**   Used to separate items in a series. Used before a coordinating conjunction that joins sentences. Used after certain introductory words and word groups. Used to set off most interrupting words and expressions.

**exclamation point**   Used to end expressions of strong feeling.

**hyphen**   Used in some spelled-out numbers. Used to link two or more words that work as a single adjective before a noun. Used to link the parts of some compound words. Used to show a break between syllables in a word broken at the end of a line of writing.

**italics**   Slanted type used to punctuate titles of long works and as emphasis. Handwriting uses underlining instead of italics.

**period**   Used to end statements, polite requests, and commands.

**semicolon**   Used to join sentences that are not connected by a coordinating conjunction. Used to join items in a series when one or more items include a comma.

**question mark**   Used to end questions.

**quotation marks**   Used to enclose a speaker's exact words and the titles of short works.

# Mini-Lessons Taught in This Book

## Acknowledgments

Grateful acknowledgment is made to the following sources for having granted permission to reprint copyrighted materials. Every effort has been made to obtain permission to use previously published materials. Any errors or omissions are unintentional.

6 Traits model. Developed by Education Northwest, 101 Southwest Main, Portland, OR 97204. http://educationnorthwest.org/traits.

Excerpt from *Mark Twain Along the Mississippi* by Wayne Youngblood. Copyright © 2006 by World Almanac Library and reprinted by permission of Gareth Stevens Publishing. Page 68.

Excerpt from "Homework Does Not = A's." *USA Today.* July 2, 2006. Reprinted with permission. Page 128.

"This Is Heaven to Me" by Carole Boston Weatherford. From *Becoming Billie Holiday* by Carol Boston Weatherford. Copyright © 2008 by Carol Boston Weatherford. Published by Wordsong, an imprint of Boyds Mills Press. Reprinted by permission. Page 192.

Book review for "Shark Girl." Used with permission of School Library Journal, Copyright © 2010. All rights reserved. Page 257.

Photograph, "A corner in an old time sweatshop." Courtesy of *New York Call Photographs,* Kheel Center, Cornell University. Page 290.

"Brazilian Experience" (p. 60), "The Guide to a Dream Date," (p. 118), "Stop Talking, Start Driving" (p. 183), "Warped Reality" (p. 249) and "*Soul Surfer* Book Review" (p. 310). Reprinted with permission of Teenink.com and *Teen Ink* magazine.

# Index

for narrative tests, 241–242

organizing ideas and details, 9–10, 25, 41, 75, 88–89, 101, 135–136, 148–150, 162, 199–200, 229, 263, 276, 293

for personal narratives, 198–200

for persuasive brochures, 161–162

for persuasive essays, 147–150

for persuasive test essays, 175

for poetry, 227–230

for a response to a DBQ, 290–293

for a response to a narrative, 261–263

for a response to a poem, 275–276

for stories, 214–216

strategies for, 112, 176

tips for, 52, 74, 112

Primary sources, 285

first-person accounts from factory workers, 288

newspaper articles, 280

photographs, 290

Pro-con charts, 176

Prompts

analyzing, 8, 24, 40, 73, 87, 99, 147, 161, 198, 214, 227, 240–241, 261, 275, 290–291, 302–303

critical-lens, 302

for a descriptive composition, 50

examples, 110, 174

for an expository test essay 110

for narratives, 240, 248

for a persuasive test essay, 174, 175

for a response to a critical-lens quotation, 309

stand-alone, 240

Pronouns, 316

Publishing, 18

Publishing articles, 47

Publishing cause-and-effect essays, 107

Publishing editorials, 142–143

Publishing essays, 94, 298

Publishing how-to articles, 81

Publishing paragraphs, 18, 269

Publishing personal narratives, 207

Publishing persuasive brochures, 169

Publishing persuasive essays, 156

Publishing poems, 236

Publishing a response to a document-based question, 298

Publishing a response to a narrative, 269

Publishing a response to a poem, 282

Punctuation, 317–318

Punctuation marks, 106, 218

**Q**

Question marks, 318

Questions

to ask a peer reviewer, 279, 295–296

asking, 66

to help with editing, 298

Quotation marks, 204, 318

Quotations, 294

response to critical-lens quotations, 301–309

writing sentences with, 294

**R**

Reading, 106

Reading documents, 291, 292

Real-world examples

of descriptive writing, 3

of literary writing, 191–192

of persuasive writing, 127–128

of response to literature, 256–257

Reference tools, 17

Response to a critical-lens quotation, 301–309

evaluating, 306, 308

rubric for, 307

strategies for organizing, 305

tip for, 305

Response to a document-based question, 285–299

assignment, 287

drafting, 293

editing, 298

evaluating, 299

getting feedback on, 295–296

model essay, 286–287, 294, 299

presentation of, 298

prewriting, 290–293

publishing, 298

revising, 295–296

rubric for, 297

traits of, 285

writing, 287, 295

Response to a narrative, 259–270

assignment, 261

drafting, 263–264

editing, 267

models, 260, 270

prewriting, 261–263

revising, 265–266

rubric for, 266

strategies to help with, 263–264

traits of, 259

Response to a poem, 271–284

assignment, 274–275

drafting, 277–278

editing, 282

evaluating, 283

getting feedback on, 279

model essay, 283–284

model passage, 272–273, 277

presentation, 282

prewriting, 275–276